ECUMENISM OF BLOOD

Ecumenism of Blood

Heavenly Hope for
Earthly Communion

Hugh Somerville Knapman, OSB

Paulist Press
New York / Mahwah, NJ

Library of Congress Cataloging-in-Publication Data
Names: Knapman, Hugh Somerville, author.
Title: Ecumenism of blood : heavenly hope for earthly communion / Hugh Somerville Knapman, OSB.
Description: New York : Paulist Press, 2018. | Includes bibliographical references and index.
Identifiers: LCCN 2018009152 (print) | LCCN 2018029570 (ebook) | ISBN 9781587687440 (ebook) | ISBN 9780809153718 (pbk. : alk. paper)
Subjects: LCSH: Martyrdom—Christianity. | Christian martyrs. | Catholic Church—Doctrines. | Catholic Church—Relations—Eastern churches. | Eastern churches—Relations—Catholic Church.
Classification: LCC BR1602 (ebook) | LCC BR1602 .K53 2018 (print) | DDC 272—dc23
LC record available at https://lccn.loc.gov/2018009152

ISBN 978-0-8091-5371-8 (paperback)
ISBN 978-1-58768-744-0 (e-book)

Published by Paulist Press
997 Macarthur Boulevard
Mahwah, New Jersey 07430

www.paulistpress.com

Printed and bound in the
United States of America

To the twenty-one Coptic martyrs

Milad Makeen Zaki
Abanoub Ayad Ateya
Maged Soliman Shehata
Youssef Shoukry Younan
Kirollos Boshra Fawzy
Bishoy Estefanous Kamel
Samuel Estefanous Kamel
Malak Ibrahim Sinyout
Tawadros Youssef Tawadros
Gerguis Milad Sinyout
Mina Fayez Aziz
Hany Abdel Mesih Saleeb
Samuel Elham Wilson
Ezzat Boushra Naseef
Luka Nagaty Anis
Gaber Mounir Adly
Essam Baddar Samir
Malak Farag Ibrahim
Sameh Salah Farouk
Gerguis Samir Megally
Mathew Ayairga (from Ghana)

Contents

Preface

IN 2017, the great paschal solemnities of Easter were affected horribly by the bombings of two Coptic Orthodox churches in Egypt by the Islamist group Daesh/ISIS on Palm Sunday. The bombers struck while the two communities were at worship, celebrating the liturgy of Christ's entry into Jerusalem that led to his passion and death on the cross. Adding to the force and poignancy of these senseless deaths of 44 people and the wounding of 118 others was the fact that this year the churches of the East and the West were celebrating the paschal feasts at the same time. For the Coptic Christians in Alexandria and Tanta that day, the commemoration of the Lord's passion became far more literal and immediate.

However, these bombings were just the latest in the ongoing suffering and persecutions endured by the Coptic Christians of Egypt. Indeed, throughout this region, Christians have faced a new, more brutal, and more determined persecution. Its leading agents are the militants of Daesh, or what is commonly called in the West, the Islamic State.[1] Elsewhere, some established states, either militantly religious or militantly atheist, are also major persecutors of Christians. Of the top ten countries in which Christians face "extreme" persecution, one is militantly atheist (North Korea) and the other nine are overwhelmingly Muslim.[2] In Iraq, attacks on Christians have increased to the point where the 1.4 million Christians there in 2003 has reduced to 275,000 in 2016.[3] In Egypt, the homeland of the Coptic church whose members make up around 10 percent of the country's population, persecution is more disjointed and opportunistic, abetted not so much by the government's policy, as by its frequent connivance, ambivalence, or, at best, indifference.[4]

It is now well attested that Christians are the most persecuted group in the world. Between 2000 and 2010, over a million Christians were murdered for their faith, at an average of over 109,000 each year.[5] In 2016, there was a relative respite with 90,000 Christians dying for their Christianity.[6] Yet as disturbing as the constant news of persecuted Christians coming from the Middle East might be, that region does not account for the majority of deaths of persecuted Christians: 70 percent of all Christians killed are in tribal Africa.[7]

Furthermore, it is estimated that from the foundation of Christianity until the year 2000, 69,420,000 Christians have been killed for their faith, and of that total, nearly two-thirds (45 million) were killed in the twentieth century.[8] Add to this the deaths so far from this century and the total exceeds seventy million.

Nevertheless, despite these persecutions, or perhaps because of them, Christianity has experienced an inexorable growth. In 1900, out of a global population of 1.62 billion people, 558 million, or 34 percent, were Christian, and by 2017 the number of Christians had grown to 2.48 billion, or 33 percent of a global population of 7.5 billion.[9] Significantly, that growth has occurred in Africa. In 1900, Africa had 8.7 million Christians[10] among a total of 97 million people,[11] making up 9 percent of the African population. By 2000, the number of Christians in Africa had risen to 360 million, and in 2017, there is an estimated 582 million[12] out of a total population of 1.25 billion,[13] now making up 47 percent of the African population.

Europe, the identity and culture of which have been inextricably intertwined with Christianity for more than a millennium and a half, offers a contrast. In 1900, out of a total population of 402 million,[14] there were 368.3 million Christians,[15] making up 92 percent of the European population. By 2017, out of a total population of 739.2 million,[16] the Christian population had reached 554.2 million,[17] making up only 75 percent of the European population. In Africa, 77 percent of Christians attend church regularly, while in Europe, regular church attendance is currently at 21 percent.[18]

While the statistics in the United States are more promising due partly to immigration, over the past century, Europe, which has been Christian historically, has experienced a decline in its Christian population in proportion to the total population while at the same time growing more affluent, and socially and technologically more progressive. In Africa, Christianity continues to grow and to be practiced at an impressive rate despite suffering by far the highest incidents of Christian persecution. These figures serve to confirm the famous adage of Tertullian (†240) that the blood of martyrs is the seed of Christians.[19] Where it is persecuted, the Christian faith tends to flourish, but where it sits comfortably in its secular context, it seems to lose its power to attract and keep its members.

A possible conclusion emerges: martyrdom offers the church an opportunity for growth in vigor and discipleship. When we are weak, then we are strong, as St. Paul teaches.

More recently, European Christians are experiencing the reality of martyrdom. In July 2016, Fr. Jacques Hamel, aged eighty-six, was in his small church near Rouen in France offering Mass when two Islamists burst into the church, and before a hastily erected video camera, slit the priest's throat. Addressing three elderly female hostages, the two men denied that Jesus was anything more than a man.[20] On Maundy Thursday, April 13, 2017, the archbishop of Rouen announced that the process to canonize Fr. Hamel had been officially commenced, four years earlier than usual by special dispensation of Pope Francis. Fr. Hamel's martyrdom may yet prove to be a blessing for the church in France, where the eldest daughter of the church is now a mere shadow of her former self.

This is ultimately a book about martyrdom. It is necessarily theological and proposes an ecumenical consequence of martyrdom not yet fully recognized nor articulated. It has been long acknowledged, at least notionally, that martyrdom builds the church; not necessarily in immediate numerical growth, but always in the holiness and faith of those who endure in the commitment to Christ and the gospel.

The book further proposes that martyrdom can enhance Christian solidarity and contribute to rebuilding the unity of the Body of Christ, the church. No one who can fulfill the requirements of perfect discipleship—to lay down one's life for Christ and with Christ—can be cut off from the Body of Christ. Christ's blood reconciled humankind to God; blood spilled for faith in him can surely reconcile anyone to the Body of Christ, even amid personal or ecclesial messiness and failure. It is no wonder that, from the beginning, Christians treasured the bloody relics of their martyrs as encouragement for their own weak faith and in acknowledgment that the martyrs are now with Christ at the right hand of the Father, pleading for all humankind.

As Western Christians grapple with the demands of a virulently secular society, the example of today's Christian martyrs calls us from debating if and how to dilute the less secular-friendly aspects of the Christian gospel that we might find a readier welcome in society, and bids us to "strive first for the kingdom of God and his righteousness, and all these things will be given to you as well" (Matt 6:33). The martyrs are a reminder that Christian discipleship always and necessarily comes at a cost. God's grace is free, but it can never be cheap.

Acknowledgments

IT WAS a conversation with Mr. Graham Hutton, National President of Aid to the Church in Need UK, that planted the seed for this book. Professor Stephen Bullivant of St. Mary's University, Twickenham, watered that seed in urging me to undertake formal research to see how far the thesis could be maintained, and after the Master of Philosophy was awarded for the dissertation, encouraged me to seek a publisher. In the intervening period, Professor Gavin D'Costa at the University of Bristol gently and wisely shepherded me as I sought, in the space of a year, to construct from the initial maelstrom of insights and intuitions a dissertation I dare to call coherent. Paulist Press graciously took the gamble to publish it, and in Mr. Paul McMahon provided a most patient, pleasant, and helpful editor. The parish of Alderney in the Channel Islands and Dr. Ralph and Mrs. Cathy Townsend offered me refuges for writing at crucial times. Without my monastic community of Douai Abbey generously allowing me to pursue this study, this book would never have seen the ink of print. Any errors in it are mine alone.

Introduction

POSING THE QUESTION

THE MURDER of twenty Coptic Christians and one Muslim Ghanaian on a Libyan beach in February of 2015 by Islamist militants aligned with Daesh received significant media attention. Many in the West gawped with macabre fascination at the highly choreographed, yet grotesque ritual of these murders filmed by Daesh for propaganda. Many were struck by the calm witness of these men as they mouthed the name of Jesus before their death. Such graphic footage emphasized the present reality of persecution and martyrdom faced by their brethren in the Middle East.

Most Christians of the Middle East belong to ancient churches, such as the Coptic Orthodox church in Egypt, which are not in formal communion with the Roman Catholic church and have their own traditions and practices. The Coptic Orthodox church moved quickly to canonize the twenty-one Libyan martyrs in their traditional way.[1] Some Catholics felt that the Copts' martyrdom should be honored also by the Catholic church,[2] at the very least to show solidarity with persecuted fellow Christians. For example, Christopher Altieri, an official at Vatican Radio, told me in personal correspondence that an impromptu shrine to the Libyan martyrs had been erected in the Gesù, the principal Jesuit church in Rome. In Catholic understanding, this is evidence of a *cultus*, one of the preconditions for canonization in the Catholic church.

Such a positive attitude toward a church still technically considered schismatic, and even heretical, by the Catholic church cannot be dismissed as some manifestation of an unrealistic and starry-eyed ecumenism. Pope Francis, publicly though informally, referred to the Libyan Copts as "martyrs," invoking several times the concept of an "ecumenism of blood," which he had identified even before the martyrdom of the Copts.[3] However, while many were supportive of the papal desire for solidarity with other persecuted Christians, some saw in his remarks a dangerous innovation with doctrinal and ecclesiological implications that rendered them at best unfeasibly idealistic, and at worst heretical.[4]

The reality of Christianity as the most persecuted religion in the world today, seen in light of the ecumenical project endorsed and encouraged by the Second Vatican Ecumenical Council (hereafter, Vatican II),[5] seems to require that Pope Francis's unsystematic yet emphatic response to the Coptic martyrs be systematically investigated. Respect for his office as supreme pastor of the churches in communion with the Holy See of Rome would by itself require such consideration, quite apart from the ecumenical imperative articulated by Vatican II (1962–65), which has been given a new urgency by contemporary persecution. The blood of the martyrs has been a seed for the growth of the church from the beginning of Christianity.[6] No less today, martyrs' blood should be the seed for the growth of a reunified church. Herein lies the potential of the ecumenism of blood.

ANSWERING THE QUESTION

This work is an initial step toward a systematic theological investigation of the dimensions of the ecumenism of blood within the context of Roman Catholic doctrine. It seeks to answer first the question, *Can the principle of ecumenism of blood be reconciled with Catholic doctrine?* Consequently, the Coptic martyrs of Libya are a case study in the practical application of the ecumenism of blood and thereby endeavor to answer a second question: *Can the Catholic church formally recognize the Coptic Orthodox church's canonization of the twenty-one martyrs of Libya?*

In answering this question, the concept of *reconciliation by blood* will be considered. This concept is derived by analogy with the long-established doctrine of baptism by blood. In theological enquiry, analogy tests a proposition for consistency with what is already firmly believed and accepted, to establish "the coherence of the truths of faith among themselves and within the plan of revelation."[7] Such an *analogia fidei* ("analogy of faith") ensures that any proposed development does not involve a contradiction of revealed truth but only a deepened understanding of truth.[8] It is as a "heuristic principle which [can lead] to the discovery of new insights"[9] that *analogia fidei* is being employed.

Thus, reconciliation by blood is proposed by analogy with baptism of blood as a legitimate development or elaboration of the established doctrine of martyrdom and its effects. At its heart is a revealing parallel between, on the one hand, sacramental baptism by water and sacramental absolution of sin, and, on the other hand, baptism by blood and reconciliation by blood. Sacramental baptism both removes inherited sinfulness and establishes the new Christian within the communion of the Catholic church. Sacramental reconciliation absolves postbaptismal personal sin and reestablishes the Christian in the personal communion with the church, which was first established at baptism. Analogously, therefore, I propose that, as baptism by blood also removes inherited sinfulness and establishes the unbaptized martyr in communion with the church, reconciliation by blood for non-Catholic Christians reconciles them to full communion with the church that was, in fact, established at their sacramental baptism.

The phenomena of heresy and schism have disturbed the Christian church and its mission since its earliest days. Patristic and subsequent conciliar teaching denied any efficacy to the martyrdom of those judged as heretics or schismatics. We will examine this Catholic doctrinal status quo, as invoked by the critics of Pope Francis and the ecumenism of blood, which denies recognizing schismatics and heretics the fruits of their martyrdom, and then determine how Catholic teaching should be applied in the contemporary context, especially regarding an evolving relationship with the Coptic church and other ancient churches. I argue that when the contemporary context is examined more closely, the traditional doctrine does not generally apply to members of the Coptic Orthodox church.

The historical determination by the Catholic church that the Oriental churches, of which the Coptic Orthodox is one, are heretics will be shown to be no longer sustainable considering recent statements on the Christological issues previously held to separate the two churches. The removal of heresy allows, at least theoretically, for an easier resolution of the enduring schism between the two churches.

Although the schism between the Coptic Orthodox and Catholic churches endures on a formal level, I argue that the Coptic martyrs of Libya need not be denied formal recognition as martyrs by the Catholic church. The argument recognizes the significantly divergent historical context in which the original denial of recognition was made. The patristic teaching, and the subsequent magisterial affirmation of it, had been predicated on the active, free, and deliberate, or contumacious, choice by schismatics to adopt a position that removed them from communion with the Catholic church.

However, in the modern context, members of the churches that emerged from such ancient schisms have not made a similarly deliberate choice against the Catholic church. They inherit the faith that has been handed on to them by the local church in their sociocultural context. Inheriting both faith and denomination, they understand themselves quite naturally and in good faith to be within that "one, holy catholic and apostolic church" of the creed. In effect, we find an intra-Christian manifestation of the theological principle of invincible ignorance normally used for unevangelized non-Christians. Once again, by analogy, the concept of *inculpable schism* will be proposed regarding Christians such as the Coptic Orthodox as an elaboration of the doctrine of invincible ignorance. To do this, I will apply the insights of eighteenth-century theologian Prospero Lambertini, later elected Pope Benedict XIV, and of Professor Stephen Bullivant.

With this understanding of the contemporary theological and ecclesiological situation and considering the implications and applications of the dogmatic principles of baptism of blood and inculpable schism, I will argue that the Coptic Orthodox Christian today must be regarded from a Catholic perspective as being in inculpable schism. In other words, rather than being denied formal recognition as a martyr, a Coptic Orthodox Christian who is murdered for his faith in Christ can now be formally recognized as a martyr by the Catholic church. A Copt who is killed because of Christ's name will have achieved the disciple's highest conformity to Christ, and thus to Christ's Body, the church. The non-Catholic martyr, reconciled by the blood of martyrdom, will have been reconciled with the universal church through the highest act of love and discipleship possible for any Christian.

It is the principle of reconciliation by blood proposed here that offers a doctrinal opening to allow for formal recognition of the Coptic Orthodox martyrs by the Catholic church. While the Catholic church cannot canonize members of other churches, and would not seek to do so, it can still incorporate saints from other churches into its worship by employing the mechanism of equivalent canonization. The current pope and his predecessor have both employed this mechanism. In a particularly relevant example, Pope Francis employed the mechanism of equivalent canonization to the Armenian, St. Gregory of Narek, who died outside formal communion with the Catholic church.

This book examines, first, the recent emergence and understanding of the theological principle of the ecumenism of blood. It then considers the understanding of martyrdom in the Catholic tradition up to the papacy of Pope Francis. Following this is a discussion of the development of the doctrine of baptism by blood and the role of sacramental reconciliation as the remedy for serious postbaptismal sin. From this, it will be argued that reconciliation by blood, as restoring communion with the Catholic church in a way analogous to sacramental reconciliation, is consistent with Catholic doctrine.

Essential to this discussion is a critical examination of the principal traditional objection to Catholic recognition of non-Catholic martyrs, namely that martyrdom confers no benefit to the schismatic or heretic. I will argue that Coptic Orthodox martyrs certainly meet the primary criterion for martyrdom: death inflicted in hatred of Christ. Moreover, it will be argued that the disqualification from martyrdom that applies to heretics and schismatics would not apply to the Coptic Orthodox martyrs of Libya, since the Catholic church does not now apply the judgment of schism or heresy to the inculpable non-Catholic. Instead, for the Coptic Orthodox martyr, the grace of martyrdom would be as that of sacramental reconciliation, restoring communion with the Catholic church through martyrdom, the perfect act of Christian discipleship.

Consequently, I will argue that there is no doctrinal impediment to the Catholic church's formal, liturgical recognition of the Coptic Orthodox canonization of the martyrs of Libya. In fact, to enable such recognition, I will propose the mechanism of equivalent canonization, especially given its recent application to a saint who died technically outside formal communion with the Catholic church and its subsequent positive ecumenical reception. Formal Catholic recognition of the Coptic Orthodox[10] canonization of the Libyan martyrs would constitute a confirmation and application of the ecumenism of blood, and significantly advance the ecumenical project to which the Catholic church is committed for the benefit of all Christians.

1

Understanding the Ecumenism of Blood

POPE FRANCIS AND THE PERSECUTION OF CHRISTIANS

ON SEVERAL occasions, publicly though not systematically, Pope Francis has used the unfamiliar phrase "ecumenism of blood." He has done so in response to increasingly alarming reports of Christians, both Catholic and non-Catholic, being killed for their Christianity, especially in the Middle East. His use of the term grew more emphatic after the deaths of the Copts in Libya, though he had first used it more than a year before their deaths.

In December 2013, responding to a question regarding the priority of ecumenism from Andrea Tornielli, the Vatican correspondent for the Italian newspaper, *La Stampa*, Pope Francis said,

> Yes, for me ecumenism is a priority. Today there is an ecumenism of blood. In some countries they kill Christians for wearing a cross or having a Bible and before

they kill them they do not ask them whether they are Anglican, Lutheran, Catholic, or Orthodox. Their blood is mixed. To those who kill we are Christians. We are united in blood, even though we have not yet managed to take necessary steps towards unity between us and perhaps the time has not yet come. Unity is a gift that we need to ask for. I knew a parish priest in Hamburg who was dealing with the beatification cause of a Catholic priest guillotined by the Nazis for teaching children the catechism. After him, in the list of condemned individuals, was a Lutheran pastor who was killed for the same reason. Their blood was mixed. The parish priest told me he had gone to the bishop and said to him: "I will continue to deal with the cause, but both of their causes, not just the Catholic priest's." This is what ecumenism of blood is. It still exists today; you just need to read the newspapers. Those who kill Christians don't ask for your identity card to see which Church you were baptized in. We need to take these facts into consideration.[1]

Pope Francis recognized the contemporary situation in which Christians of all denominations are being persecuted without reference to their denomination but only to their profession of faith in Christ. This represents for him a kind of unity, not a formal unity for which the "necessary steps" have yet to be taken, but a material unity in blood. He implies that this promotes formal unity, which is "a gift that we need to ask for." Pope Francis has refocused the ecumenical initiative away from the formal, institutional unity being laboriously investigated by theologians to an informal, grassroots, and immediate unity in the martyr-blood of ordinary Christians.

Several months later, Francis invoked the ecumenism of blood without explicitly employing the term. In an address to the Armenian catholicos, Karekin II, he spoke this time of an "ecumenism of suffering":

Your Holiness, dear Brothers, the sufferings endured by Christians in these last decades have made a unique and invaluable contribution to the unity of Christ's disciples. As in the ancient Church, the blood of the martyrs became the seed of new Christians. So too in our time the blood of innumerable Christians has become a seed of unity. The ecumenism of suffering and of the martyrdom of blood are a powerful summons to walk the long path of reconciliation between the Churches, by courageously and decisively abandoning ourselves to the working of the Holy Spirit. We feel the duty to follow this fraternal path also out of the debt of gratitude we owe to the suffering of so many of our brothers and sisters, which is salvific because it is united to the Passion of Christ.[2]

Martyrdom is again cast as a pan-Christian phenomenon, one that is to be understood as "a seed of unity" and a "powerful summons" to pursue "reconciliation between the Churches." It is significant that he ended this address with a quotation from the Armenian theologian and saint Gregory of Narek.

Later the same year, Pope Francis spoke again of the ecumenism of blood in an address to members of the charismatic movement at the Vatican:

Spiritual ecumenism is praying and proclaiming together that Jesus is Lord, and coming together to help the poor in all their poverty. This must be done while never forgetting in our day that the blood of Jesus, poured out by many Christian martyrs in various parts of the world, calls us and compels us towards the goal of unity. For persecutors, we are not divided, we are not Lutherans, Orthodox, Evangelicals, Catholics...No! We are one in their eyes! For persecutors we are Christians! They are not interested in anything else. This is the ecumenism of blood that we experience today....

> Spiritual ecumenism and the ecumenism of blood.
> The unity of the Body of Christ. Prepare the Bride for
> the Bridegroom who comes! One Bride only![3]

Pope Francis states what will become a consistent, if undeveloped, theme in his presentation of the ecumenism of blood. The indiscriminateness with which persecutors attack Christians effects a real if passive ecumenical unity: "For persecutors we are Christians! They are not interested in anything else. This is the ecumenism of blood we experience today." Second, he locates "spiritual ecumenism and the ecumenism of blood. The unity of the Body of Christ" in an eschatological context, invoking the imagery of the Book of Revelation (22:17): "Prepare the Bride for the Bridegroom who comes! One Bride only!" It can be reasonably inferred that Francis sees more in the ecumenism of blood than a means to restore temporal, formal unity, but as something inevitably linked to the eschatological mission of the church.

In one of the more important statements on the ecumenism of blood, Pope Francis issued a joint declaration with Bartholomew, patriarch of Constantinople, in October 2014. Once again the term "ecumenism of suffering" is employed synonymously for ecumenism of blood, and again martyrdom is seen as a seed for growth toward unity:

> As Saint Paul reminds us, "If one member suffers, all suffer together; if one member is honored, all rejoice together" (1 Cor 12:26). This is the law of the Christian life, and in this sense we can say that there is also an ecumenism of suffering. Just as the blood of the martyrs was a seed of strength and fertility for the Church, so too the sharing of daily sufferings can become an effective instrument of unity.[4]

St. Paul's teaching must be seen in the context of his assumption that there can be no isolation among Christians who are members of Christ's Body. It is a communion in which the suffering of "one member" of the Body of Christ affects "all." That the pre-eminent prelates of the Western and Eastern churches together quote this Pauline teaching implies a mutual recognition that there is a degree of achieved communion between them, particularly through "the law of Christian life." This allows for an "ecumenism of suffering," which has the potential to be "an effective instrument of unity."

The term "ecumenism of blood" itself was not used in this joint declaration. At this stage of its development, it is an exclusively Catholic, and particularly papal, term. In Patriarch Bartholomew's separate address to Pope Francis on the same day, he nevertheless accepts some of the principles informing the ecumenism of blood. He agrees that persecutors have no concern for denominational differences among the Christians whom they persecute, and that through "the blood of martyrdom" the very "unity that concerns us is regrettably already occurring."[5] Patriarch Bartholomew's address, as well as the joint declaration itself, implies that Pope Francis's teaching on the ecumenism of blood is being received by the Orthodox even in its undeveloped state.

Two months later, Pope Francis returned briefly but emphatically to the ecumenism of blood in his homily at the solemn vespers of the Feast of the Conversion of St. Paul celebrated at the Basilica of St. Paul Outside the Walls in Rome:

> In this moment of prayer for unity, I would also like to remember our martyrs, the martyrs of today. They are witnesses to Jesus Christ, and they are persecuted and killed because they are Christians. Those who persecute them make no distinction between the religious communities to which they belong. They are Christians and for that they are persecuted. This, brothers and sisters, is the ecumenism of blood.[6]

This brief statement contains certain elements that are becoming consistent marks of the ecumenism of blood, particularly that

persecutors "make no distinction" between Christian denominations.

DAESH/ISIS

Less than a month later, the highly publicized murder of
twenty Coptic men and one Muslim man on a Libyan beach,[7]
and their brief but clear profession of faith in Christ before their
execution, moved Pope Francis to revisit the principle of ecumenism of blood when addressing the moderator of the Church
of Scotland on the latter's visit to the Vatican:

> Today I read about the execution of those twenty-one
> or twenty-two Coptic Christians. Their only words
> were: "Jesus, help me!" They were killed simply for the
> fact that they were Christians. You, my brother, in your
> words referred to what is happening in the land of Jesus.
> The blood of our Christian brothers and sisters is a testi-
> mony which cries out to be heard. It makes no difference
> whether they be Catholics, Orthodox, Copts or Protes-
> tants. They are Christians! Their blood is one and the
> same. Their blood confesses Christ. As we recall these
> brothers who died only because they confessed Christ,
> I ask that we encourage each another to go forward with
> this ecumenism which is giving us strength, the ecumen-
> ism of blood. The martyrs belong to all Christians.[8]

Pope Francis reiterated that the profession of faith in Christ is
the common denominator for establishing a unity in blood, and
that martyrs' blood is itself a fundamental confession of faith in
Christ. This allows an ecumenism in blood because "the martyrs
belong to all Christians."

A further papal statement on the ecumenism of blood was
prompted by another tragic slaughter the following April. Daesh
beheaded or shot twenty-eight Ethiopian Orthodox Christians

whom they had abducted in Libya. Again, the murders were recorded by Daesh on video for propaganda. In response, Pope Francis wrote to the patriarch of the Ethiopian Orthodox church, Abuna Matthias:

> I know that Your Holiness is suffering deeply in heart and mind at the sight of your faithful children being killed for the sole reason that they are followers of our Lord and Saviour Jesus Christ....
>
> It makes no difference whether the victims are Catholic, Copt, Orthodox or Protestant. Their blood is one and the same in their confession of Christ! The blood of our Christian brothers and sisters is a testimony which cries out to be heard by everyone who can still distinguish between good and evil.[9]

Although the term is not used, the ecumenism of blood clearly underlies the pope's statement. Familiar elements of it recur here: the persecutors' disregard for denominational difference, and the blood of the victims as a confession of faith in Christ. To this was added a third element: that the blood of martyrs is an evangelical witness to the world, to "everyone who can still distinguish between good and evil."

THE CONTEXTUALIZATION OF DISUNITY

The next month, on May 10, 2015, in a formal message to the Coptic patriarch Tawadros II, on the second anniversary of their meeting, Pope Francis gave further shape to the emerging form of the ecumenism of blood:

> Today more than ever we are united by the ecumenism of blood, which further encourages us on the path

towards peace and reconciliation. I assure you and the Christian community in Egypt and throughout the Middle East of my unceasing prayer, and I remember in particular the Coptic faithful recently martyred for their Christian faith. May the Lord welcome them into his Kingdom.

With thanksgiving to the Lord, I recall our advances along the path of friendship, united as we are by one baptism. Though our communion is yet imperfect, what we have in common is greater than what divides us. May we persevere on our journey to full communion, and grow in love and understanding.

It is particularly encouraging that the Joint International Commission for Theological Dialogue between the Catholic Church and the Oriental Orthodox Churches has recently finalized the document *The Exercise of Communion in the Life of the Early Church and its Implications for our Search for Communion Today*.[10]

Pope Francis affirmed that the twenty-one victims of Daesh in Libya were "martyred" rather than merely murdered. In doing so, he accepted that they died not for a denomination but "for their Christian faith." By such common witness to faith in Christ, Copts and Catholics are "united by the ecumenism of blood," a yet incomplete unity that "further encourages us on the path towards peace and reconciliation," which are still to be fully established since "our communion is imperfect." Nevertheless, both churches are "united...by one baptism," and what they "have in common is greater than what divides" them. This growing contextualization of disunity is significant, for it excludes any sense of an absolute and irretrievable disunity.

Equally deserving consideration here is the fact that Francis situates this contextualization of disunity in relation to the report of an official theological dialogue between the Catholic and Coptic churches, which was to be published three days later: "The Exercise of Communion in the Life of the Early Church and Its

Implications for Our Search for Communion Today."[11] This document was the fruit of systematic theological discussion and its treatment of martyrdom (Section IV, nos. 33–44) can be seen as foundational for the concept of ecumenism of blood. It identifies martyrdom as a "common mark of all churches since early Christianity" and "a part of the churches' mission," and affirms that "Martyrs belong to the core of the church" (no. 33). It also maintains that Christ "unites all who believe in Him through baptism in one body" (no. 36). Martyrdom is a form of evangelization since "from the life and death of the martyrs a light falls on central truths of life and faith" (no. 37). The martyr is considered bound to "the sacramental dimension of the Church" in such a way as to embody it and fulfill it:

> What is represented in the form of signs in the sacrament becomes concrete reality in their lives. Everything that is granted to believers in baptism can be given to the unbaptized true believer through martyrdom. (no. 39)

Most significant of all is its understanding of martyrdom in relation to ecclesial communion and the sacrament of baptism:

> Since the early days of Christianity, martyrdom has been a unique sign of communion. The entire Church has understood and considered those who were not yet baptized but became martyrs for the name of Christ as great saints. The church in both East and West called it the "baptism of blood."
>
> Not only do the fathers see martyrdom as analogous to baptism, to some it even appears more filled with grace than baptism, as St. Cyprian of Carthage wrote: "Can the power of baptism be greater or of more avail than confession, than suffering, when a person confesses Christ before men and is baptized in his own blood?" (Ep. 72,21) And further: "they certainly

are not deprived of the sacrament of baptism who are baptized with the most glorious and greatest baptism of blood, concerning which, the Lord also said that He 'had another baptism to be baptized with.' [Lk 12:50] But the same Lord declares in the Gospel that those who are baptized in their own blood and sanctified by suffering are perfected" (Ep. 72,22). (nos. 40–41)

This is significant first for its explicit affirmation of the equivalence of martyrdom, as "baptism of blood," with sacramental baptism in establishing the martyr in communion with the universal church, and it does so by employing analogy. Indeed, it implicitly approves Cyprian's view of the superiority of martyrdom as "the most glorious and greatest baptism of blood." Yet it is equally significant for what was *omitted* from the quotation from Cyprian's Epistle 72:

And yet even this baptism does not benefit a heretic, although he has confessed Christ, and been put to death outside the Church...[for] not even the baptism of a public confession and blood can profit a heretic to salvation, because there is no salvation out of the Church.[12]

THE CASE OF THE COPTS

The Coptic church was one of a few small but ancient churches (termed Oriental Orthodox) that did not accept the definitions of the Council of Chalcedon (451) on the nature of Christ, particularly the council's condemnation of monophysitism and its adoption of a dyophysite understanding of Christ. As a result, the Copts were considered by the Chalcedonian churches (including the Catholic church) as implicitly monophysite and thus heretical. However, in the twentieth century, a rapprochement between the two churches led to a revision of this assumption.

The Catholic church accepted the Coptic claim to be miaphysite rather than monophysite when it cosigned the Catholic–Coptic *Common Report and Brief Formula* issued by both churches in 1988. Here, they jointly professed a common belief in the nature of Christ.[13] In referencing the document produced by the Catholic-Oriental joint commission and its use of St. Cyprian's teaching, Pope Francis has implicitly confirmed this doctrinal resolution. Heretical teaching is no longer an issue in the relationship between the Catholic and Coptic churches. All that remains now is a state of formal schism.[14]

Despite the reality of schism, the document "The Exercise of Communion" concludes on a highly positive note. It sees that most of the elements that constituted the communication and communion shared by Copts and Catholics prior to Chalcedon are still to be found today. These include the exchange of visits between the heads of the churches, shared prayer and shared veneration of the saints, common pilgrimages, exchanges between monastic communities, and formal presence at each other's synods and significant liturgical events.[15] In light of this fact, the Commission resolved to "examine in a positive way remaining divergences in doctrine and practice" with a view to "asking themselves to what extent a restoration of the relationships that existed in the early centuries would be sufficient to restore full sacramental communion today," including a "consideration of the place of the Bishop of Rome in that communion."[16] It seems reasonable to view Pope Francis's advocacy of the ecumenism of blood as a contribution to the project of restoring communion between the two churches, and furthermore, as evidence of the positive role of the Bishop of Rome.

A few weeks later, on July 3, 2015, Pope Francis added more substance to the concept of ecumenism of blood. In a public address to a gathering in St. Peter's Square, he spent considerable time on ecumenism. He maintained that the divisions between Christians are "a counter-testimony," which must be offset by various modes of practical ecumenism: "spiritual ecumenism, the ecumenism of prayer, the ecumenism of work, but of charity at

the same time; the ecumenism of reading the Bible together";
and, finally, the ecumenism of blood:

> Unity, for the blood of today's martyrs makes us one.
> There is the ecumenism of blood. We know that when
> those who hate Jesus Christ kill a Christian, before kill-
> ing him, they do not ask him: "Are you a Lutheran, are
> you an Orthodox, are you an Evangelical, are you a Bap-
> tist, are you a Methodist?" You are Christian! And they
> sever the head. They are not confused; they know there
> is a root there, which gives life to all of us and which is
> called Jesus Christ, and that it is the Holy Spirit who
> leads us to unity! Those who hate Jesus Christ, led by
> the Evil One, do not confuse one with the other. They
> know and therefore kill without asking questions.
>
> And this is something that I entrust to you, per-
> haps I have already told you this, but it is a true story.
> It is a true story. In Hamburg, a city of Germany, there
> was a parish priest who studied the writings to carry
> forward the cause for the beatification of a priest killed
> by Nazis, guillotined. The reason: he taught children
> the catechism. And, as he studied, he discovered that
> after the priest, five minutes later, a Lutheran pastor
> was guillotined for the same reason. And the blood of
> both was mixed: both were martyrs, both were mar-
> tyrs. It is the ecumenism of blood. If the enemy unites
> us in death, who are we to be divided in life? Let us
> allow the Spirit to enter, let us pray to go forward all
> together. "But there are differences!" Let us leave them
> aside; let us walk with what we have in common, which
> is enough: there is the Holy Trinity; there is Baptism.
> Let us go forward in the strength of the Holy Spirit.
>
> A few months ago, there were those 23 [*sic*] Egyp-
> tians who were also beheaded on the beach in Libya,
> who in that moment said Jesus' name. "But they were
> not Catholics...." But they were Christians, they are

brothers, they are our martyrs!—the ecumenism of blood. Fifty years ago, at the canonization of the young martyrs of Uganda, Blessed Paul VI made reference to the fact that their Anglican companion catechists had also poured out their blood for the same reason; they were Christians, they were martyrs. Excuse me, do not be scandalized, they are our martyrs! Because they gave their life for Christ and this is the ecumenism of blood—pray, remembering our common martyrs.[17]

Although it is not formal teaching, on several occasions, as noted throughout this chapter, Francis identifies and affirms some of the attributes and consequences of the ecumenism of blood. He boldly states that the blood of the martyrs "makes us one," reaffirming a material unity already attained among the Christian communities that he recognized in his message two months earlier to the Coptic pope, Tawadros II, and in his 2013 interview with Andrea Tornielli. The persecutors, he says, make no distinction as to denomination, they "do not confuse one with the other." It is the unity in the profession of faith in Jesus Christ that is the motivation for the persecution of Christians.

In the final part of the section just quoted, Pope Francis refers specifically to the Copts executed in Libya for their Christian faith and invokes "the ecumenism of blood" to justify claiming them as "our martyrs." He offered the fundamental criterion for the ecumenism of blood, saying that the martyrs "gave their life for Christ and this is the ecumenism of blood." This came after a reference to Pope Paul VI's canonization in 1964 of the Catholic martyrs of Uganda, who died alongside Anglicans who were specifically mentioned by Pope Paul VI.[18] For Pope Francis, these Anglicans, though not canonized formally, have equal significance since "they were Christians, they were martyrs....do not be scandalized, they are our martyrs." Pope Francis moved beyond the restrained and discreet reference to the Anglicans by Pope Paul VI in 1964 and explicitly acknowledged the Anglicans as fellow martyrs with the Catholics.

THE LÜBECK MARTYRS

As previously noted, Pope Francis made an intriguing reference to a priest in Hamburg who was advancing the cause for canonization of another Catholic "priest" who, along with a Lutheran pastor, was guillotined by the Nazi authorities for teaching the catechism. He names neither of them, but drew a significant conclusion from their example, namely that "the blood of both was mixed: both were martyrs, both were martyrs. It is the ecumenism of blood. If the enemy unites us in death, who are we to be divided in life?" Pope Francis told substantially the same story in his interview with *La Stampa* in December 2013 cited earlier, when he added the detail that the priest promoting the Catholic martyr's cause told his bishop he would continue to do so only if he could promote the cause of the Lutheran as well.[19]

While Pope Francis never refers to the martyrs by name, it seems that he is referring to the Lübeck Martyrs,[20] three young Catholic priests—Hermann Lange, Eduard Müller, and Johannes Prassek—and an older Evangelical Lutheran pastor—Karl Stellbrink—who were guillotined in quick succession on November 10, 1943, in a Hamburg prison. They had become friends and collaborators a couple of years earlier. Their crime, in the eyes of the Nazi authorities, had been more serious than merely teaching the catechism. They had been circulating the sermons of the bishop of Münster, Blessed Clemens von Galen, which denounced, among other things, Gestapo terror and the Nazi program of euthanasia against the disabled. The four men had also been publicly questioning the legitimacy of Germany's war. Eyewitnesses to their beheading reported that their blood was mixed together and flowed as one stream from the guillotine.[21]

Their deaths as well as their ministry were beacons of ecumenical hope. A fellow prisoner, Adolf Ehrtmann, who survived the war, was adamant that the four martyrs should be remembered together and not separated according to denomination:

"Never say three, always say four!" Pope Benedict said before the beatification of the three priests in 2011:

> The Beatifications of Georg Häfner in Würzburg, as well as of Johannes Prassek, Hermann Lange and of Eduard Müller in Lübeck, will take place in the coming year. The Evangelical Pastor Karl Friedrich Stellbrink will also be commemorated, together with the Chaplains of Lübeck. The attested friendship of four clerics is an impressive testimony of the ecumenism of prayer and suffering which flourished in various places during the dark period of Nazi terror. We can look to these witnesses as luminous indicators for our common ecumenical journey.[22]

Pope Benedict identified an "ecumenism of prayer and suffering," a term that echoes Pope Francis's own use of these terms as noted earlier. The eyewitness testimony that the blood of the Catholics and the Lutheran mixed and flowed together seems to be the inspiration for Pope Francis's own repeated claim for Christian martyrs of whatever denomination: "Their blood is mixed." As with the Ugandan martyrs, the non-Catholic martyr was mentioned and commemorated as far as was possible at the beatification of the Catholics.

These actions and words of two recent popes, Paul VI and Benedict XVI, affirm that Pope Francis's advocacy of ecumenism of blood has not emerged from nothing. However, the groundwork for the acts of these popes can be found as far back as the work of an eighteenth-century theologian who would later become Pope Benedict XIV. It is appropriate now to observe the full sweep of Catholic teaching on martyrdom to appreciate how the ecumenism of blood has blossomed.

2

The Catholic Doctrine
of Martyrdom

THE TEACHING OF CHRIST

SINCE IT is proposed that the ecumenism of blood is consistent with, and flows from, Catholic doctrine, it is timely to survey briefly the relevant aspects of Catholic teaching on martyrdom. The official *Catechism of the Catholic Church* defines *martyrdom* as:

> The supreme witness given to the truth of the faith:
> it means bearing witness even unto death. The martyr
> bears witness to Christ who died and rose, to whom he
> is united by charity. He bears witness to the truth of
> the faith and of Christian doctrine. He endures death
> through an act of fortitude. (no. 2473)

The martyr is one who witnesses to Christ to the point of accepting a death like Christ's motivated by a courage born of faith. Therefore, the martyr does not die merely for the sake of conscience;

the martyr dies because of faith in and adherence to Christ. In the days of pagan persecution, this was a harsh but straightforward reality for Christians. The heresies of the early church, and later the onset of the Protestant Reformation, complicated Christian martyrdom by introducing the unhappy situation of Christians dying at the hands of other Christians due to conflicting understandings of Christ's teaching and its implications. Martyrdom, therefore, began to include not only the fundamental endurance of death inflicted because of faith in Christ, but also because of "the truth of the faith and of Christian doctrine," dying for Christ and for true faith in Christ.

It is in Christ's own teaching that the high status of martyrdom is revealed, related as it is to his crucifixion and resurrection. First, he taught his disciples that "if any want to become my followers, let them deny themselves and take up their cross and follow me. For those who want to save their life will lose it, and those who lose their life for my sake will find it" (Matt 16:24–25).

It would be an inevitable feature of the life of the Christian church, even if not necessarily for every individual Christian, that "they will hand you over to be tortured and will put you to death, and you will be hated by all nations because of my name" (Matt 24:9). In the Book of Revelation, John hears the Lord address the situation of the infant church facing persecution:

> Do not fear what you are about to suffer. Beware, the devil is about to throw some of you into prison so that you may be tested, and for ten days you will have affliction. Be faithful until death, and I will give you the crown of life. (Rev 2:10)

In the Sermon on the Mount, Christ identified an essential mark of the Christian martyr: the martyr does not retaliate when persecuted, nor seeks revenge: "But I say to you, Do not resist an evildoer. But if anyone strikes you on the right cheek, turn the other also" (Matt 5:39). Instead, the persecuted is to return love for persecution, an act that shares in divine perfection: "But I say

17

to you, Love your enemies and pray for those who persecute you, so that you may be children of your Father in heaven....Be perfect, therefore, as your heavenly Father is perfect" (Matt 5:44–45a, 48).

Last, Christ interprets his own sacrificial death as a martyrdom, which he links to baptism: "I have a baptism with which to be baptized, and what stress I am under until it is completed!" (Luke 12:50). Christ is the archetype and perfection of martyrdom, the model and the inspiration for Christian martyrs. To do as Christ did and love as he loved is to obey Christ perfectly and be more fully conformed to him, for "no one has greater love than this, to lay down one's life for one's friends. You are my friends if you do what I command you" (John 15:13–14).

The martyr accepts the call of Christ to share in his sufferings and self-sacrifice on the cross in a literal, suprasacramental way, both as an act of personal devotion, but also, as St. Paul teaches, as a service to the church:

> I am now rejoicing in my sufferings for your sake, and
> in my flesh I am completing what is lacking in Christ's
> afflictions for the sake of his body, that is, the church.
> (Col 1:24)

What is lacking in Christ's sufferings is not, of course, some deficiency in Christ's sacrifice but that his sacrifice is yet fully and completely to suffuse the whole of his Body, the church, and become manifestly and fully integral to its identity before the world.

BAPTISM OF BLOOD

Not surprisingly, this New Testament teaching forms Catholic teaching on martyrdom. The Catholic church develops this teaching by identifying certain conditions that must be fulfilled for martyrdom to be authentically Christian. There are three essential conditions, which may be summarized as physical death, inflicted in hatred of Christ and Christian teaching, and voluntarily accepted:

> Those...were seen to be truly martyrs...who had fulfilled the "conditions" for martyrdom. In the first place, one had to lay down one's physical life and really experience death. Second, death had to be the result of hatred of the life and truth proclaimed by christian [*sic*] teaching. Last, such a death had to be voluntarily accepted in witness to and defense of christian values.[1]

To be a Christian martyr, it is not necessary to be a baptized Christian, only that one has faith in Christ and at least implicitly desires to be baptized. In the persecutions of the early church, those under instruction for baptism were sometimes executed before they could be baptized. In these cases, the church allowed that martyrdom was for them a type of baptism and imparted the justifying grace of baptism: their sins were forgiven, and they "were considered to have been initiated into the christian [*sic*] community by a 'baptism of blood.'"[2]

It should be noted, however, that baptism by blood does not confer a sacramental character as does baptism by water.[3] Since sacramental character is ordered to the Christian's life on earth, this lack of the sacramental character in baptism by blood means it does not have the "ecclesiological effect" of establishing membership in the church militant, "which exists as a sign of God's kingship on earth," but it does establish "conformity with Christ dying in sacrifice out of love for the Father"[4] and so it establishes the martyr in the heavenly Body of Christ, the church triumphant. It is the sacramental grace of justification that is the effect of baptism by blood. The significance of this distinction will be clarified later.

The recognition of the capacity of martyrdom to effect a baptism in blood dates from the early church. The earliest extant reference to martyrdom's baptismal equivalence is to be found in a fragment of the writings of Melito of Sardis (†180):

> For two things constitute provision for the forgiveness
> of sins: suffering for Christ, and baptism.[5]

Melito's teaching finds many echoes among other patristic authorities. Tertullian (†240) taught that martyrdom was a second mode of baptism that could both introduce the effects of sacramental baptism and restore the effects of sacramental baptism if they had been lost through grave sin, such as apostasy:

> We have indeed, likewise, a second font, (itself withal one with the former,) of blood....This is the baptism which both stands in lieu of the fontal bathing when that has not been received, and restores it when lost.[6]

Cyprian of Carthage (†258) also taught the baptismal effect of martyrdom for unbaptized catechumens:

> They certainly are not deprived of the sacrament of baptism who are baptized with the most glorious and greatest baptism of blood, concerning which the Lord also said, that He had another baptism to be baptized with. But the same Lord declares in the Gospel, that those who are baptized in their own blood, and sanctified by suffering, are perfected.[7]

The *Apostolic Tradition* attributed to Hippolytus of Rome (†235) confirms the power of martyrdom to justify the unbaptized martyr:

> If a catechumen should be arrested for the name of the Lord, let him not hesitate about bearing his testimony; for if it should happen that they treat him shamefully and kill him, he will be justified, for he has been baptized in his own blood.[8]

The baptismal effect of martyrdom is consistent with the understanding that emerged from the beginning of the Christian church that martyrdom was the highest conformity to Christ, a profound sharing in his identity and mission. Martyrdom has always been essential to and inseparable from Christianity. In a sense, the earthly mission of Christ was to be a martyr, and so Christ stands as the inspiration, model, and archetype for the Christian martyr, and martyrdom becomes the perfection of life in Christ. Ignatius of Antioch (†108) prayed for the grace of martyrdom so "that I may not merely be called a Christian, but really found to be one" for only in martyrdom "shall I truly be a disciple of Christ."[9]

MARTYRDOM AND CHURCH

In recent times, martyrdom has been the focus of renewed attention, not least due to the two world wars and the phenomenon of state-sponsored persecution on an industrial scale. This trend confirms the high status given to martyrdom in the church's tradition, agreeing with "the primitive Church [that] Christian perfection and martyrdom were practically identical terms, so that the martyr represents the first class of Saints."[10]

Vatican II confirmed the exalted status of martyrdom:

> The Church, then, considers martyrdom as an exceptional gift and as the fullest proof of love. By martyrdom a disciple is transformed into an image of his Master by freely accepting death for the salvation of the world—as well as [by] his conformity to Christ in the shedding of his blood. (*Lumen Gentium* 42)[11]

Moreover, the inseparability of martyrdom from the nature and mission of the church is such that "martyrdom, thus, belongs to the essence of the Church," and indeed, "Church and martyrdom testify to each other reciprocally."[12]

While martyrdom does not confer a sacramental character, it does effect a real relationship to the church. As previously noted, it conforms the martyr to Christ in his heavenly body rather than his earthly body, the church triumphant rather than the church militant. Nevertheless, even from an earthly perspective, the church recognizes the witness of the martyr as relevant to its own identity. Craig Hovey speaks of martyrdom as a "mark of the church."[13] Given that Christ and the church, his Body, are indivisible, and given that sacramental baptism is made into the death and resurrection of Christ, Hovey concludes that martyrdom, as a material sharing in the death and resurrection of Christ, inevitably has an ecclesial significance:

> To identify with Christ in his death and resurrection *is* to identify with the church. But this also makes sense only if the church is a martyr-church....To die with Christ is not just to "die to sin." It is also to be realigned with a new people created by God for life in the kingdom in which Christ reigns supreme.[14]

Hovey is careful to locate the end of martyrdom "in the kingdom in which Christ reigns supreme," while at the same time allowing that there must be some relation to the earthly community "created by God for life in the kingdom." That relation he situates in martyrs' identification with the church through their shared identification with Christ's death and resurrection—the martyr in a literal way, the church in a sacramental way—so that the church of the baptized is also the "martyr-church." While the martyr may not have been a baptized member of the church, through martyrdom the martyr shares in its faith in Christ, as well as in its evangelical mission as a witness both to Christ and to the church's relationship with Christ. This interpretation finds some confirmation in Christ's words: "John said to him, 'Teacher, we saw someone casting out demons in your name, and we tried to stop him, because he was not following us.' But Jesus said, 'Do not stop him; for no one who does a deed of power in my name will be able soon afterward to speak evil of me. Whoever is not against us is for us'" (Mark 9:38–40).

Against this understanding of martyrdom being a baptism by blood for the unbaptized must be set the limitations on recognizing martyrdom regarding those who had already been baptized. Founded on the apostles, the church held the apostolic power to determine the truth with authority, the power to bind and to loose (Matt 18:18), meaning that the church could legitimately claim to speak with the voice of Christ: "Whoever listens to you listens to me, and whoever rejects you rejects me, and whoever rejects me rejects the one who sent me" (Luke 10:16).

Therefore, the death of Christians at the hands of heretical Christians for adhering to apostolic truth became another instance of authentic Christian martyrdom. Furthermore, those Christians who remained obstinate in heresy or defied the authority of the church became ineligible for authentic Christian martyrdom. To be put to death for Christ was not the full story. For the baptized, faith in Christ required communion with his Body, the church. Those who willfully set themselves against the teaching or the authority of the church could not, therefore, be Christian martyrs, however conscientious their deaths. Augustine offered the classic statement of the principle involved, that it is the cause more than the death that makes the martyr:

> Therefore Martyrs not the punishment but the cause makes, for if punishment made Martyrs, all the mines would be full of Martyrs, every chain would drag Martyrs, all that are executed with the sword would be crowned. Therefore let the cause be distinguished; let none say, because I suffer, I am righteous. Because He who first suffered, suffered for righteousness' sake, therefore He added a great exception, Blessed are they which are persecuted for righteousness' sake.[15]

Another North African, Cyprian of Carthage, was equally adamant that neither the heretic nor the schismatic could die as martyrs, for their separation from the church was a denial of the perfection of love intrinsic to martyrdom:

Even if such men were slain in confession of the Name, that stain is not even washed away by blood: the inexpiable and grave fault of discord is not even purged by suffering. He cannot be a martyr who is not in the Church; he cannot attain unto the kingdom who forsakes that which shall reign there. Christ gave us peace; He bade us be in agreement, and of one mind. He charged the bonds of love and charity to be kept uncorrupted and inviolate; he cannot show himself a martyr who has not maintained brotherly love.[16]

A later father, Fulgentius of Ruspe (†533), is possibly even more emphatic in denying the status of martyr to heretics and schismatics, even to denying them the possibility of salvation:

Believe strongly and without a doubt, that any heretic or schismatic, baptized in the name of the Father and of the Son and of the Holy Spirit, absolutely cannot be saved if he is not a member of the Catholic Church, however generous his alms may be, and even if he sheds his blood for the name of Christ. For all those who do not remain in unity with the Church cannot attain salvation, despite being baptized, and despite their almsgiving, abundant though it may be, and even despite their suffering death for the name of Christ, if they persist in the error, whether heretical or schismatic, which leads to death.[17]

The higher authority of church councils confirmed these teachings of individual fathers. The Council of Laodicea (c. 363) considered as false martyrs and unworthy of Christian veneration those heretics who had been killed in persecution:

No Christian shall forsake the martyrs of Christ, and turn to false martyrs, that is, to those of the heretics, or those who formerly were heretics; for they are aliens

24

from God. Let those, therefore, who go after them, be anathema.[18]

Much later, the fifteenth-century Council of Florence, in its *Decree for the Copts* (1442), again denied both the status of martyr and indeed salvation to heretics and schismatics, explicitly citing Fulgentius:

> [The holy Roman church] firmly believes, professes, and preaches that "no one remaining outside the Catholic Church, not only pagans," but also Jews and heretics or schismatics, can become partakers of eternal life; but they will go to the "eternal fire prepared for the devil and his angels" (Mt 25:41) unless before the end of their life they are joined to it. For union with the body of the Church is of so great importance that the sacraments of the Church are helpful to salvation only for those remaining in it; and do fasts, almsgiving, and other works of piety, and exercises of a militant Christian life bear eternal rewards for them alone. "And no one can be saved, no matter how much alms he has given, even if shedding one's blood for the name of Christ, unless one remains in the bosom and unity of the Catholic Church."[19]

The uncompromising wording of this decree allows apparently no room for maneuver in its detailed list of those excluded from salvation, and in categorically denying any fruit to the martyrdom or other meritorious works of those outside the Catholic church "unless before the end of their life they are joined to it." The various fathers and councils were seeking to deal with those who were making an active and willful decision to "forsake" the doctrine, and so also the communion, of the church. However, it does not explicitly consider the case of one who has not actively and freely chosen to forsake the church and its teaching. The fathers and the councils left unexamined the possibility that "shedding one's blood in the name of Christ" might itself be a means of reconciliation with the church triumphant in heaven, if perhaps not explicitly with the church militant on earth, for those Christians who, at the moment of death, were outside the communion of the church not by their own wrong choice but by the force of circumstance.

3

A Developing Doctrine

HERESY AND SCHISM

IT HAS been seen that the early church exalted martyrdom,
allowing that it baptized the unbaptized who were murdered in
hatred of Christ. Yet we have seen that the baptized Christian
who was cut off from the communion of the church through
heresy or schism could not be accepted as a true martyr, a
teaching that prevailed without nuance until the Council of
Florence in the fifteenth century. By the eighteenth century,
however, with the heresies and schism of the Reformation having
taken root, theologians began to perceive an inadequacy in the
accepted articulation of the doctrine on martyrdom, especially
regarding those who were schismatics by reason of their birth
into a particular sociocultural context. It is the Catholic church's
engagement with this reality that led to an increasingly generous
approach to those Christians who were born into separation from
it. The fruit of this development came at the Second Vatican
Council and the teaching of the postconciliar popes, providing
fertile soil for Pope Francis's ecumenism of blood.

Despite the vehemence of patristic language, it is important to understand that no heretic or schismatic is considered necessarily cut off from the church forever. The Catholic church considers them rather as prodigals whose proper home remains in Catholic communion. This understanding has been enshrined in the church's canon law:

> In the first Christian excommunications...the offender is cut off from the Christian community to compel him to mend his ways....[Excommunication] now operates to separate the delinquent not from the Church, to which he is definitively attached by baptism, but from the communion of the faithful. That is to say, he is deprived of a number of rights.[1]

The consistent penalty for both heresy and schism is excommunication.[2] This penalty, like other penalties, is not intended by the Catholic church to be vengeful but medicinal:

> They have a threefold object—punishment of the offender, protection of the common good, and reformation of the transgressor.[3]

However, context is important here. Canon law has in mind those who by a conscious, deliberate, and responsible act contumaciously choose a position opposed to the faith and discipline of the Catholic church. With new heresies and schisms emerging frequently in the life of the church, such deliberate choices were often to be made. With the passage of time, some groups that were separated from the church came to have a life of their own, from one generation to another. This fact posed a question: are those who are born into schismatic Christian churches to be treated as equivalent to contumacious schismatics? Canon law, after all, presumes *contumacy*, that is, a deliberate, free, and obstinate choice for heresy or schism.[4]

In fact, the current canon law of the Catholic church has

faced this issue. It groups the three offenses against the teaching authority of the church together:

> Heresy is the obstinate denial or obstinate doubt after the reception of baptism of some truth which is to be believed by divine and Catholic faith; apostasy is the total repudiation of the Christian faith; schism is the refusal of submission to the Supreme Pontiff or of communion with the members of the Church subject to him.[5]

An English-language commentary on canon law interprets this canon in a way that reflects the expanded ecumenical horizons of Vatican II:

> The concepts of heresy, apostasy, and schism must be viewed within the framework of communion, the several elements of which are detailed in *Lumen gentium* 14 and 15 and in *Unitatis redintegratio* 3. Christians are joined together by much more than the profession of common doctrine, not the least of which unifying factors is charity. Indeed the terms heresy, apostasy, and schism are no longer used of those born and baptized outside the visible communion of the Catholic Church. The offences can be ascribed only to Catholics, those baptized into the Catholic Church or later received into it.[6]

CONTUMACY AND "ORIGINAL SCHISM"

Those who inherit rather than actively choose a historical state of separation from the Catholic church are exonerated, in a juridical sense, of heresy or schism. These crimes can only be ascribed to those who are formally and fully in communion with the Catholic church and who make a deliberate, free, and obstinate—that is, contumacious—choice to reject the faith or communion of the church. On the face of it, this should absolve those who inherit rather than choose schism, as well as heresy, from the church's traditional negative judgment on the salvific or evangelical value of their murder in hatred of Christ.

This interpretation of canon 751 makes explicit reference to the teaching of Vatican II in two of its documents. The first is *Lumen Gentium*:

> The Church recognizes that in many ways she is linked with those who, being baptized, are honored with the name of Christian, though they do not profess the faith in its entirety or do not preserve unity of communion with the successor of Peter....They are consecrated by baptism, in which they are united with Christ....Likewise we can say that in some real way they are joined with us in the Holy Spirit, for to them too He gives His gifts and graces whereby He is operative among them with His sanctifying power. Some indeed He has strengthened to the extent of the shedding of their blood. (no. 15)

The Catholic church here affirms that those baptized outside the visible communion of the Catholic church are nevertheless united with Christ, whose Spirit is at work among them in "sanctifying power." More importantly, it recognizes that non-Catholic Christians can be "strengthened to the extent of shedding their blood," implicitly allowing for non-Catholic martyrs.

The second conciliar document by which canon 751 is interpreted, *Unitatis Redintegratio*, requires more extensive quotation due to its relevance here:

> Even in the beginnings of this one and only Church of God there arose certain rifts, which the Apostle strongly condemned. But in subsequent centuries much more

serious dissensions made their appearance and quite large communities came to be separated from full communion with the Catholic Church—for which, often enough, men of both sides were to blame. The children who are born into these Communities and who grow up believing in Christ cannot be accused of the sin involved in the separation, and the Catholic Church embraces upon them as brothers, with respect and affection. For men who believe in Christ and have been truly baptized are in communion with the Catholic Church even though this communion is imperfect....It remains true that all who have been justified by faith in Baptism are members of Christ's body, and have a right to be called Christian, and so are correctly accepted as brothers by the children of the Catholic Church.

Moreover, some and even very many of the significant elements and endowments which together go to build up and give life to the Church itself, can exist outside the visible boundaries of the Catholic Church: the written word of God; the life of grace; faith, hope and charity, with the other interior gifts of the Holy Spirit, and visible elements too. All of these, which come from Christ and lead back to Christ, belong by right to the one Church of Christ.

The brethren divided from us also use many liturgical actions of the Christian religion....These liturgical actions must be regarded as capable of giving access to the community of salvation.

It follows that the separated Churches and Communities as such, though we believe them to be deficient in some respects, have been by no means deprived of significance and importance in the mystery of salvation. For the Spirit of Christ has not refrained from using them as means of salvation which derive their efficacy from the very fullness of grace and truth entrusted to the Church. (no. 3)

This long quotation contains many of the elements of the council's approach to non-Catholic Christians. Those born into communities historically separated from the Catholic church "and who grow up believing in Christ cannot be accused of the sin involved in the separation, and the Catholic Church embraces them as brothers," because there is nothing contumacious in their separation. Theirs is a sort of original schism, analogous to original sin: inherited, not personally willed. Moreover, those who have been "truly baptized are in communion with the Catholic Church even though this communion is imperfect," and are "members of Christ's body." Therefore, valid baptism in any Christian denomination establishes a real if imperfect communion with the Catholic church. Elements of grace, and so also manifestations of God's presence, are to be found in these separated Christian communities, and such elements are ordered to unity with the Catholic church because they "come from Christ and lead back to Christ, [and] belong by right to the one Church of Christ." The worship of these separated communities is "capable of giving access to the community of salvation," and "the Spirit of Christ has not refrained from using them as means of salvation which derive their efficacy from the very fullness of grace and truth entrusted to the Church." The Catholic church does not consider non-Catholic denominations to be empty vessels.

This new generosity of tone in acknowledging the real if inadequate communion of non-Catholic Christians with the Catholic church may appear a radical departure from the more uncompromising teaching found in the fathers and the earlier councils. Yet it is not so much a departure as an increased awareness and comprehension of the historical reality of separation of some communities from the Catholic church, "for which, often enough, men of both sides were to blame" (*Unitatis Reditegratio* 3), and that "children born into those communities today are not to be accused of the sin involved in separation."[7] In other words, the context and circumstances of non-Catholic denominations are now more actively and attentively acknowledged. That this is a doctrinal development rather than a novelty can be seen by noting an element in the tradition in which Vatican II's teaching finds foundation.

PROSPERO LAMBERTINI, BENEDICT XIV

In the early twentieth century, the Dominican René Hedde addressed the issue of "heretic or schismatic false martyrs."[8] He distinguishes between two cases: the heretic who dies because of his heresy, and the one who is killed because of a doctrine he holds in common with the Catholic faith. Having taken the first case as obviously incompatible with Catholic recognition of martyrdom, Hedde explores the "more interesting second case"[9] by referring to the teaching of Cardinal Prospero Lambertini (later Pope Benedict XIV, 1740–58) in his treatise of 1737, *De Servorum Dei Beatificatione et Beatorum Canonizatione* (On the Beatification of Servants of God and the Canonization of the Beatified).[10] Hedde examines Lambertini's question as to whether one he calls the invincible heretic (*l'hérétique invincibiliter*) can be an authentic martyr. In other words, can one who is a non-Catholic Christian "in good faith" and is put to death because of an article of faith shared with the Catholic church be a true martyr?

Hedde alerts us to Lambertini's distinction in answering the question. Lambertini, he notes, concedes that an invincible heretic, provided that he was habitually disposed to believe anything proposed by legitimate teaching authority (i.e., "of good faith"), would be a martyr *coram Deo* ("in the eyes of God") but not *coram Ecclesia* ("in the eyes of the Church"), because the church would necessarily be reduced to vain speculation on the inner faith of the invincible heretic from without.[11] Hedde concludes this section with the observation that "one can see from these examples how the concept of martyrdom that, at first sight, seems very clear and sharply defined, in reality poses a number of questions which are difficult to answer with certainty."[12]

Lambertini's treatise is important here for introducing the category of invincible heretic, which is analogous to the Catholic doctrine of invincible ignorance. This latter concept was proposed by Aquinas to clear of sin the one who "fails to know what he is unable to know [but yet bound to know]...ignorance of such like things is called 'invincible'...no invincible ignorance is a sin."[13] This was given magisterial assent in Pius IX's encyclical *Singulari Quidem*,[14] and more fully and specifically in his later encyclical, *Quanto Conficiamur Moerore*.[15] Hedde understood that this development raises some questions not hitherto addressed.

In Vatican II's *Lumen Gentium*, the term "invincible ignorance" is not explicitly used though the concept is clearly present. *Lumen Gentium* 16 speaks of those "who through no fault of their own do not know the Gospel of Christ or His Church"—*sine culpa ignorantes*. Stephen Bullivant sees in this a conciliar acceptance of "inculpable ignorance" and interprets it as a development of Pius IX's teaching on invincible ignorance, itself a development of Thomistic teaching.[16] The change in adjective allows for a distinction between the impossibility of knowing on the part of the individual concerned (invincibility), as implied in Aquinas, and the infeasibility of the individual's knowing the truth if its proclamation is "either intrinsically insufficient or if Christians themselves fail scandalously (in the full, scriptural sense of the term) to live up to the name."[17]

The Catholic church accepts that the invincibly ignorant are inculpable, or blameless, for their lack of faith. By analogy, the invincible heretic—and by logical extension, the invincible schismatic—cannot be blamed for continuing in inherited heresy or schism if he has not been presented with the Catholic faith in a manner adequate to his circumstances. Combining the insights of Lambertini and Bullivant, we might therefore speak of non-Catholic Christians of good faith as inculpable heretics or schismatics.

It might be suggested that, based on Lambertini's teaching alone, it is conceivable that an inculpable heretic or schismatic could be recognized as a martyr by the Catholic church, both *coram*

Deo and *coram Ecclesia*. The condition imposed by Lambertini for recognition before God is that before his death the invincible heretic had been "habitually disposed to believe anything proposed by legitimate teaching authority."[18] It can be reasonably assumed that this condition would be fulfilled by the person's willing submission to the teaching authority of his own denomination, which would be for him, to the best of his knowledge in his inculpable separation from the Catholic church, a "legitimate teaching authority." It seems reasonable to conclude that this would be a sufficient measure of the "good faith" necessary, in Lambertini's view, for a martyr's recognition both *coram Deo* and *coram Ecclesia*, as it entails a freedom from that contumacy that is censured in canon law.

THE CHRISTOCENTRICITY OF MARTYRDOM

One other relevant aspect of Lambertini's treatise—especially significant given that it was republished during the author's subsequent pontificate as Benedict XIV—is his definition of *martyrdom*, based on the teaching of St. Augustine: "Martyrdom bears witness to the truth of divine faith, and is the voluntary endurance of death on account of faith in Christ or some other act of virtue in relation to God."[19] The significance of this definition is that it does not measure martyrdom by explicit reference to individual articles of the faith or doctrines of the Catholic church, but more fundamentally and traditionally with reference to "faith in Christ."

Vatican II's *Lumen Gentium* 4 takes up this Christocentric approach to martyrdom. The martyr is one who can show "no greater love" than in laying down "his life for Christ and His brothers," and martyrdom is declared the "fullest proof of love," which transforms the disciple into "an image" of Christ through his "conformity to Christ in the shedding of his blood." Moreover, it holds martyrdom to be also a "profession of faith." The council sees martyrdom as an exalted act of discipleship that unites the martyr with Christ such that he becomes an image of Christ. It is a unity achieved by charity and faith. Significantly, *Lumen Gentium* does not restrict this possibility to Catholics, or those in communion with the Catholic church, but is content to allow martyrdom as a possibility for "Christians." It does not labor this point, but by orienting martyrdom to faith in Christ without absolutely or explicitly requiring an adherence to a particular ecclesial community, it develops the implications of Lambertini's teaching and allows for the increasingly wider vision of martyrdom in subsequent teaching.

This wider vision can be seen in papal acts even before the end of the Second Vatican Council. In 1964, Pope Paul VI canonized St. Charles Lwanga and his twenty-one companions, who were martyred in 1886 by Mwanga II of Buganda, in what is now Uganda. Murdered alongside the twenty-two Catholics were nine Anglicans. Paul VI did not, and could not, canonize these non-Catholics, but he offered a tentative recognition of them as martyrs when he declared that their death "in the name of Christ" was "deserving mention."[20]

Later in the same homily, Paul VI makes a stronger reference to the Anglicans killed alongside the Catholics:

> And besides, to these could be added a twofold and lengthy catalogue of the others who had been killed in the same bloody persecution; on the one hand the Catholic neophytes and catechumens, and on the other the Anglicans who, so it is said, were killed on account of the name of Christ.[21]

Here, the Anglican victims are implicitly given equivalent status with catechumens, those awaiting baptism into the Catholic church. This equivalence is made somewhat ambiguously, but it remains significant. The "Catholic neophytes and catechumens" could be accounted as martyrs by the Catholic church quite easily by means of the established doctrine of baptism by blood.

However, if the Anglicans (apparently not neophytes but baptized) are of equivalent status in having been killed "on account of the name of Christ," the question arises: In what way might their blood benefit them as it does the Catholic catechumens and neophytes who are baptized in their blood?

MARTYRDOM AND COMMUNION

Paul VI's successor, John Paul II, expressed at least twice a similar expansion in tone and vision regarding non-Catholic martyrs. In his Apostolic Letter *Tertio Millennio Adveniente*, he taught the following:

> At the end of the second millennium, *the Church has once again become a Church of martyrs.* The persecutions of believers—priests, Religious and laity—has caused a great sowing of martyrdom in different parts of the world. The witness to Christ borne even to the shedding of blood has become a common inheritance of Catholics, Orthodox, Anglicans and Protestants, as Pope Paul VI pointed out in his Homily for the Canonization of the Ugandan Martyrs. (no. 37)[22]

Here, John Paul II confirms Paul VI's tentative recognition in 1964 of the Anglican Christians as having been killed "in the name of Christ." He develops it further when declaring that "the witness to Christ borne even to the shedding of blood" is something that is to be considered as "a common inheritance of Catholics, Orthodox, Anglicans and Protestants." Denominational difference and ecclesial separation are set aside as factors in the recognition of martyrs. This marks another development in broadening the scope of Christian martyrdom in the teaching of the Catholic church.

A year later, John Paul II issued the encyclical *Ut Unum Sint*, subtitled in English "On Commitment to Ecumenism." In it, he articulates what was implicit in Paul VI's homily at the canonization of the Ugandan martyrs:

> I have mentioned the will of the Father and the spiritual space in which each community hears the call to overcome the obstacles to unity. All Christian Communities know that, thanks to the power given by the Spirit, obeying that will and overcoming those obstacles are not beyond their reach. All of them in fact have martyrs for the Christian faith. Despite the tragedy of our divisions, these brothers and sisters have preserved an attachment to Christ and to the Father so radical and absolute as to lead even to the shedding of blood. But is not this same attachment at the heart of what I have called a "dialogue of conversion"? Is it not precisely this dialogue which clearly shows the need for an ever more profound experience of the truth if full communion is to be attained?
>
> In a theocentric vision, we Christians already have a common *Martyrology*. This also includes the martyrs of our own century, more numerous than one might think, and it shows how, at a profound level, God preserves communion among the baptized in the supreme demand of faith, manifested in the sacrifice of life itself. The fact that one can die for the faith shows that other demands of the faith can also be met. I have already remarked, and with deep joy, how an imperfect but real communion is preserved and is growing at many levels of ecclesial life. I now add that this communion is already perfect in what we all consider the highest point of the life of grace, *martyria* unto death, the truest communion possible with Christ who shed his Blood, and by that sacrifice brings near those who once were far off (cf. *Eph* 2:13). (nos. 83–84)[23]

John Paul II has built on the insights of Lambertini/Benedict XIV, Paul VI, and Vatican II, giving them a solemn and explicit inclusivity. He acknowledged the situation of inherited, non-contumacious schism and effectively confirmed the possibility of Lambertini's invincible heretic.[24] He allows that all Christian communities have "martyrs for the Christian faith," since despite ecclesial separation, there were some who "preserved an attachment to Christ and to the Father so radical and absolute as to lead even to the shedding of blood." "In a theocentric vision," standing for what Lambertini termed *coram Deo*, Christian communities share "a common Martyrology" or a communion of martyrs, which shows "how, at a profound level, God preserves communion among the baptized in the supreme demand of faith, manifested in the sacrifice of life itself."

Most significantly, the exalted status and ecumenical efficacy of martyrdom are affirmed emphatically when John Paul II teaches that martyrdom is the "highest point of the life of grace," which manifests a "communion [that] is already perfect," which is "the truest communion possible with Christ" whose own self-sacrifice "brings near those who once were far off." There is no ambiguity or tentativeness in the papal language here. In martyrdom, inculpable non-Catholic Christians of good faith achieve a perfect communion with the church in their "truest...possible" communion with Christ that is the fruit of martyrdom. It seems reasonable to allow that Lambertini's condition of "good faith" is more than satisfied in "an attachment to Christ and to the Father [that is] so radical and absolute."

A NEW TEACHING?

At first sight, this might appear to some as a complete reversal of the traditional Catholic recognition of martyrs as set forth in the previous chapter. It is, in fact, a recognition that ongoing ecclesial disunity is generally passively and inculpably received by the non-Catholics who inherit it rather than contumaciously chosen by them. This recognition was signaled most clearly in Vatican II's avoidance of the categories of heretic and schismatic regarding those who inherit ecclesial separation through no fault of their own—an attitude subsequently enshrined in Catholic canon law. In the absence of contumacy in ecclesial separation from the Catholic church, the pre-Lambertini denial of authentic martyrdom to heretics or schismatics, though still valid for the culpably contumacious, is not applicable to the inculpable schismatic now recognized and more adequately comprehended in recent doctrinal reflection.

In fact, not only can inculpable schismatics who are killed because of their faith in Christ now be considered equivalent to Catholic martyrs, their martyrdom is placed in the context of an "imperfect but real communion...preserved and...growing at many levels of ecclesial life." That there are "levels of ecclesial life" implies that they are objective and to some degree discernible in earthly terms (*coram Ecclesia*) since this "imperfect but real communion...[in] ecclesial life" that John Paul II recognizes exists in ways that "I have already remarked."

What John Paul II "remarked" on can be found in sections 11–14 of *Ut Unum Sint*, where he specifically invokes *Lumen Gentium*. Here the pope teaches that "the elements of sanctification and truth present in the other Christian Communities, in a degree which varies from one to the other, constitute the objective basis of the communion, albeit imperfect, which exists between them and the Catholic Church" (*Ut Unum Sint* 11).

He then quotes *Lumen Gentium*'s "elements of sanctification and truth" (no. 15) in other ecclesial communities that constitute the "objective" basis of real if imperfect communion: reverence for Scripture, worship of the Trinity, baptism, sacraments and (for some) episcopacy, Marian devotion, the shedding of blood for Christ, and, in the Orthodox churches, the celebration of the Eucharist (*Ut Unum Sint* 12). The encyclical quotes approvingly the other conciliar document of particular relevance, *Unitatis*

Redintegratio, especially its recognition that "all those justified by faith through Baptism are incorporated into Christ. They therefore have a right to be honored by the title of Christian and are properly regarded as brothers and sisters in the Lord by the sons and daughters of the Catholic Church" (*Ut Unum Sint* 13). The conclusion of these sections is particularly germane:

> These are extremely important texts for ecumenism. It is not that beyond the boundaries of the Catholic community there is an ecclesial vacuum. Many elements of great value (*eximia*), which in the Catholic Church are part of the fullness of the means of salvation and of the gifts of grace which make up the Church, are also found in the other Christian Communities.
>
> All these elements bear within themselves a tendency towards unity, having their fullness in that unity....In accordance with the great Tradition, attested to by the Fathers of the East and of the West, the Catholic Church believes that in the Pentecost Event God has *already* manifested the Church in her eschatological reality, which he had prepared "from the time of Abel, the just one." This reality is something already given. Consequently we are even now in the last times. The elements of this already-given Church exist, found in their fullness in the Catholic Church and, without this fullness, in the other Communities. (*Ut Unum Sint* 13–14)

The recognition that many "elements" of the "fullness of the means of salvation" found in the Catholic church are also found in other denominations, and that these only find fullness in communion with the Catholic church with which they have a "tendency towards unity," is predicated on the tradition of both Eastern and Western churches that the "eschatological reality" of the church has been "already manifested," and as a reality "already given." In other words, the imperfect communion between the churches is already manifest, and of its nature it is directed toward perfect communion by its "tendency towards unity." That the means of salvation are in part already visible in other Christian communities implies that the communion is not only visible "in a theocentric vision" (*coram Deo*) but also in an anthropocentric vision (*coram Ecclesia*). In other words, the imperfect communion among Christian communities that is inherently directed toward perfect communion can be recognized on earth. In the martyrs of all denominations, we can find such a manifestation of the unity and communion toward which all the elements of grace in the churches tend.

Considering *Ut Unum Sint*, it seems reasonable to set aside Lambertini's reticence in allowing the invincible/inculpable heretic or schismatic to be recognized as a martyr in the eyes of the church (*coram Ecclesia*), while allowing it in the sight of God (*coram Deo*). Separated Christians are no longer counted as heretics or schismatics *coram Ecclesia* insofar as their separation is not contumacious. By virtue of the fact that their baptism has justified them, incorporated them into Christ, and made them the brethren of Catholics, it is no longer necessary to indulge in vain speculation about the inner faith of the inculpable heretic from without.[25] For in martyrdom, the imperfect ecclesial communion of those of good faith is shown to be "already perfect" as "the truest communion possible with Christ who shed his Blood, and by that sacrifice brings near those who once were far off" (*Ut Unum Sint* 84). According to the teaching of John Paul II, martyrdom makes perfect the previously imperfect communion of those inculpably separated in good faith, and does so in the church's sight as well as God's.

Consequently, there seems to be no impediment in Catholic doctrine to allowing that non-Catholic martyrs of good faith enter, through the blood of their martyrdom, into full communion with the Catholic church. Therefore, the recent remarks of Pope Francis about the ecumenism of blood are almost inevitable within the trajectory of teaching previously set by Lambertini/ Benedict XIV, Vatican II, Paul VI, and John Paul II.

4

The Sacramentality of Blood

CATHOLIC TEACHING on the relationship of members of non-Catholic churches with the Catholic church has developed such that those who inherit "original schism" and who are of good faith are inculpable of responsibility for their separation from the Catholic church. As a result, the judgment denying the recognition of martyrdom to heretics and schismatics killed because of their faith in Christ should not apply in their case, since only Catholics who contumaciously separate themselves from communion with the Catholic church are censured for heresy or schism. Moreover, by their baptism and their recourse to the other elements of grace within their own churches, non-Catholics inculpably separated from the Catholic church are in a real though imperfect communion with it, since these same "elements bear within themselves a tendency towards unity, having their fullness in that unity" (*Ut Unum Sint* 14). In this enriched understanding of the relationship of inculpable non-Catholics of good faith with the Catholic church, we can now say, with John Paul II, that "this communion is already perfect in what we all consider the highest point of the life of grace, *martyria* unto death, the truest communion possible with Christ who shed his Blood, and by that sacrifice brings near those who once were far off" (no. 84).

BLOOD IN THE BIBLE

We need now to articulate more fully how this enriched understanding enables the ecumenism of blood. The key is in the name itself: ecumenism of *blood*.

In the Book of Genesis, after Adam and Eve's primordial sin and their consequent expulsion from paradise, the first sin presented is that of the murder of the righteous Abel by his brother Cain. God confronts Cain, saying, "What have you done? Listen; your brother's blood is crying out to me from the ground! And now you are cursed from the ground, which has opened its mouth to receive your brother's blood from your hand. When you till the ground, it will no longer yield to you its strength; you will be a fugitive and a wanderer on the earth" (Gen 4:10–12).

The blood that is spilled is depicted as both the substance of the crime and its condemnation. In the Catholic tradition, it is the first among the sins that cry to heaven for vengeance.[1] The blood of Abel can cry out and be heard because his blood is a type of Christ:

> That the blood is the Word, is testified by the blood of Abel, the righteous interceding with God. For the blood would never have uttered a voice, had it not been regarded as the Word: for the righteous man of old is the type of the new righteous one; and the blood of old that interceded, intercedes in the place of the new blood. And the blood that is the Word cries to God, since it intimated that the Word was to suffer.[2]

The Old Testament emphasizes the precious value of blood by identifying it with the principle of life within the human person. In Leviticus, God calls blood the "life of every creature" and so forbids his people to consume it lest they be "cut off": "For the life of every creature—its blood is its life; therefore I have said to the people of Israel: You shall not eat the blood of any creature, for the life of every creature is its blood; whoever eats it shall be cut off" (Lev 17:14).[3]

This prohibition was still being enforced early in the life of the Christian church when Gentile converts were also forbidden to consume blood.[4] Moreover, so important is blood as the life principle that God institutes blood sacrifice as the means for atonement and reconciliation: "For the life of the flesh is in the blood; and I have given it to you for making atonement for your lives on the altar; for, as life, it is the blood that makes atonement" (Lev 17:11).

Blood is integral to the sacrificial system that, by Moses's time, occupied "an essential and central part of Israel's religion."[5] Moses offers an example when he offered sacrifice on behalf of Israel to bring peace, and uses the blood of the sacrificed animals in a liturgy of purification of the people:

> He sent young men of the people of Israel, who offered burnt offerings and sacrificed oxen as offerings of well-being to the LORD. Moses took half of the blood and put it in basins, and half of the blood he dashed against the altar. Then he took the book of the covenant, and read it in the hearing of the people; and they said, "All that the LORD has spoken we will do, and we will be obedient." Moses took the blood and dashed it on the people, and said, "See the blood of the covenant that the LORD has made with you in accordance with all these words." (Exod 24:5–8)

Furthermore, in Exodus 12, it was by the sign of blood that the chosen people of God were delivered from slavery in Egypt and became a free nation. With God preparing to strike down all the firstborn in Egypt, through Moses he directs the Hebrews to daub the lintels of their doorways with the blood of a spotless (i.e., fit for sacrifice) lamb that had been cooked for a vigil meal, in order that they be both spared from divine wrath and able to escape from Egypt: "The blood shall be a sign for you on the houses where you live: when I see the blood, I will pass over you, and no plague shall destroy you when I strike the land of Egypt. This day shall be a day of remembrance for you. You shall celebrate it as a festival to the LORD; throughout your generations you shall observe it as a perpetual ordinance" (Exod 12:13–14). The Passover (or *Pascha* in Latin) is foundational in the identity of the people of Israel as a holy people who have been given a claim on God's mercy.

Just as Abel's blood was a type of Christ's blood, so too the sacrificial system of the old covenant is a type of the new covenant, the perfect covenant to be made in the blood of Christ who offered himself as a sacrifice to purify, reconcile, and deliver Israel, and indeed all humanity, in a final and perfect Passover. The sacrifice of Jesus is placed in a liturgical context at the Last Supper, held during the annual Jewish celebration of Passover:

> Then he took a loaf of bread, and when he had given thanks, he broke it and gave it to them, saying, "This is my body, which is given for you. Do this in remembrance of me." And he did the same with the cup after supper, saying, "This cup that is poured out for you is the new covenant in my blood." (Luke 22:19–20)

The Letter to the Hebrews interprets the sacrifice of Christ as fulfilling and completing the ritual blood sacrifices of the old covenant to establish a new and final covenant:

> But only the high priest goes into the second [tent, the Holy of Holies], and he but once a year, and not without taking the blood that he offers for himself and for the sins committed unintentionally by the people....
> But when Christ came as a high priest of the good things that have come...he entered once for all into the

Holy Place, not with the blood of goats and calves, but with his own blood, thus obtaining eternal redemption. For if the blood of goats and bulls, with the sprinkling of the ashes of a heifer, sanctifies those who have been defiled so that their flesh is purified, how much more will the blood of Christ, who through the eternal Spirit offered himself without blemish to God, purify our conscience from dead works to worship the living God!

For this reason he is the mediator of a new covenant, so that those who are called may receive the promised eternal inheritance....Not even the first covenant was inaugurated without blood. For when every commandment had been told to all the people by Moses in accordance with the law, he took the blood of calves and goats, with water and scarlet wool and hyssop, and sprinkled both the scroll itself and all the people, saying, "This is the blood of the covenant which God has ordained for you." And in the same way he sprinkled with the blood both the tent and all the vessels used in worship. Indeed, under the law almost everything is purified with blood, and without the shedding of blood there is no forgiveness of sins. (Heb 9:7, 11–15, 18–22)

In the new covenant, blood achieves its sacramental purpose, bringing to an end the sacrificial system of the old covenant and establishing a new system, not of repeated sacrifices but of a sharing in Christ's own single blood offering that cries to God now not for vengeance, as did Abel's blood, but "that those who are called may receive the promised eternal inheritance" (Heb 9:15). The church continually applies the blood offering of Christ to the church, in the sacrament of the Eucharist.[6]

Before Christ, it was by circumcision—itself a blood rite— that one was incorporated into the covenantal relationship of God with his chosen people; after Christ, baptism replaces circumcision as the means of incorporation into the new covenantal relationship.[7] In the old covenant, circumcision enabled a sharing in the deliverance granted at Passover, while in the new covenant, baptism enables a sharing in the new Passover of the Eucharist.

RECONCILIATION BY BLOOD

As previously noted, however, there is a second way to share in the new covenantal relationship: the blood of martyrdom, which brings about the same deliverance, purification, and identification with Christ as sacramental baptism. Even more, the blood of martyrdom not only attains the same incorporation into Christ as baptism, it effects a eucharistic communion with Christ in his paschal self-offering:

> The Christian who offers his life in martyrdom enters into full communion with the Pasch of Jesus Christ and thus becomes Eucharist with him. (*Sacramentum Caritatis* 85)[8]

Benedict XVI confirms John Paul II's teaching that "communion is already perfect in what we all consider the highest point of the life of grace, *martyria* unto death, the truest communion possible with Christ who shed his Blood, and by that sacrifice brings near those who once were far off" (*Ut Unum Sint* 84). The blood of martyrdom is not only a form of baptism for those not yet in the church; it is also, for those Christians who are "far off" due to their impaired communion with the Catholic church, a restoration of full communion with the church. With this comes admission to the fullness of eucharistic communion with the church by means of "the truest communion possible with Christ" in the blood of his Pasch that is attained in the blood of martyrdom. Benedict, writing as a theologian, maintains,

> The martyr lives, and gives life, above all through his death, and thus he has himself entered into the eucharistic mystery. Martyrdom is the source of faith.[9]

48

Based on this, we would be justified in understanding martyrdom as the fundamental validation of faith in Christ, and as a doorway to the full and perfect communion with Christ in his eucharistic and ecclesial Body that is the grace of baptism. It can therefore be said by analogy that just as the blood of martyrdom can effect the grace of sacramental baptism for non-Christians who die for Christ, so too the blood of martyrdom effects for non-Catholic Christians of good faith the grace of sacramental reconciliation with the Catholic church.[10]

In the Catholic church, the sacrament of penance, or reconciliation, is the normative means of absolving postbaptismal sin and restoring an individual to full communion with the church, by restoring the graced state of baptism:

> Sin is before all else an offense against God, a rupture of communion with him. At the same time it damages communion with the Church. For this reason conversion entails both God's forgiveness and reconciliation with the Church, which are expressed and accomplished liturgically by the sacrament of Penance and Reconciliation.
>
> *Reconciliation with the Church is inseparable from reconciliation with God.*
>
> Christ instituted the sacrament of Penance for all sinful members of his Church: above all for those who, since Baptism, have fallen into grave sin, and have thus lost their baptismal grace and wounded ecclesial communion. It is to them that the sacrament of Penance offers a new possibility to convert and to recover the grace of justification. The Fathers of the Church present this sacrament as "the second plank [of salvation] after the shipwreck which is the loss of grace."[11]

The early church knew a longer process of penance and reconciliation, a gradual process that moved the penitent from

49

exclusion to restored communion and the full rights of membership.[12] Taking, for example, a canon of the Council of Elvira in 300 regarding repentant heretics seeking reconciliation with the Catholic church, we also find a partial recognition of inculpability, in this case for children of contumacious heretics:

> If someone leaves the Catholic Church and goes over to a heresy, and then returns again, it is determined that penance is not to be denied to such a one, since he has acknowledged his sin. Let him do penance, then, for ten years, and after ten years may he come forward to communion. If, indeed, there were children who were led astray, since they have not sinned of their own fault, they may be received without delay.[13]

This canon makes the distinction that informs modern Catholic canon law: the parent is a heretic precisely in having chosen to leave the faith of the church; the child, having made no such choice, is exempt from penance, for the child is inculpable.

To fill out our understanding of reconciliation, we return to the teaching of the rigorist Tertullian: "We have indeed, likewise, a second font, (itself withal one with the former,) of blood....This is the baptism which both stands in lieu of the fontal bathing when that has not been received, and restores it when lost."[14] While he differed with the church over issues of practice, he agrees with the theory, that the blood of martyrdom can be baptism for the unbaptized martyr, and reconciliation for the one who has been baptized; that is, he recognizes it both effects baptism and restores it, just like the sacrament of penance.

Tertullian elsewhere in the same tract holds that sacramental baptism conferred by heretics is "not one with ours."[15] While church teaching was clear that baptism could only be received once, Tertullian advocated the rebaptism of heretics since he considered their baptism to be no baptism at all. Tertullian has in mind contumacious rather than inculpable heretics. This distinction, however, is ultimately irrelevant, as the Catholic church definitively decided against his opinion, and affirmed the validity of baptism at the hands of heretics, provided it followed the accepted form. In 256, Pope St. Stephen I (†257), writing to another great baptismal rigorist, Cyprian of Carthage, decreed,

> If therefore some come to you from any heresy whatsoever let no innovation be made except according to what has been handed down, namely let an imposition of hands be made on them by way of penance; for the heretics themselves are right in not baptising other heretics who come over to them but simply receiving them into their communion.[16]

This teaching has received consistent affirmation, notably from Pope St. Innocent I (†417), who decreed that certain heretics "should be received by the imposition of the hand only, because although they were baptized by heretics, nevertheless they were baptized in the name of Christ."[17] In 726, Pope St. Gregory II (†731) confirmed the "ancient custom of the Church" that those baptized "in the name of the Father and of the Son and of the Holy Spirit, may in no case be rebaptized."[18] On the conciliar level, the Council of Nicaea (325) confirmed that heretics seeking to return to the church needed only "the imposition of hands,"[19] and the Council of Trent (1547) anathematized those who deny the validity of baptism in the name of the Trinity conferred by heretics.[20] In fact, the Catholic church goes so far as to say that *anyone* may baptize validly, "even laymen or laywomen, or even pagans and heretics may baptize, provided they observe the Church's form and intend to do what the Church does."[21] In all cases, when the essential form is used to confer baptism, the true minister is not the priest but Christ himself. The personal status of the minister is irrelevant when it comes to a sacrament's validity.[22]

This "imposition of hands" mentioned earlier by the popes is interpreted generally as signifying the sacrament of confirmation.[23] While the imposition of hands could also signify the

51

sacrament of holy orders or the sacrament of penance, in the context of heretics validly baptized but excommunicated, and now seeking admission to the Catholic church, the logical inference is that they receive the sacrament of confirmation, that their communion "may be perfected by the imposition of hand."[24] Thus, Pope Siricius (†399) states,

> These...and other heretics we join to the Catholic assembly merely by the invocation of the septiform Spirit through the bishop's imposition of hand, as has been decided by the Synod. The same is observed everywhere in East and West.[25]

Or again, the Council of Arelas in 314, which states,

> It has been decided that, if anyone from a heretical sect come to the Church, he should be asked his creed, and if it is perceived that he has been baptized in the Father and the Son and the Holy Spirit, only the hand should be imposed upon him, in order that he may receive the Holy Spirit.[26]

However, in his judgment quoted earlier, Stephen I qualified the imposition of hands, saying "let an imposition of hands be made on them *by way of penance*." This suggests he considers the imposition of hands to be the final act in the process of reconciliation of serious sinners to the communion of the Catholic church rather than the sacrament of confirmation. Cyprian mentions this practice more than once:

> Penitence may be fulfilled in a set time, and confession may be made with investigation of the life of him who fulfils the penitence, and no one can come to communion unless the hands of the bishop and clergy be first imposed upon him.[27]

...when they have made confession, and have received the imposition of hands on them by you in acknowl-edgment of their penitence.[28]

The Third Council of Toledo (589) also confirms this understanding by invoking its antiquity:

But according to the old canons everyone who regrets his offence must be first excluded from communion, and must frequently present himself as a penitent for the laying on of hands when his time of penance is over, then, if it seems good to the bishop, he may again be received to communion.[29]

This understanding of the imposition of hands as intended for penitential absolution rather than confirmation is supported by W. A. Jurgens:

Although Stephen explicitly said *impose hands in penance*, some, thinking primarily of imposition of hands as a conferral of the Holy Spirit, and failing to distinguish between different kinds of manual impositions, under-stood that Confirmation, then joined to the baptismal rite, was to be renewed, though not, of course, the Bap-tism itself.

But Stephen did not say "the imposition of hands for the receiving of the Holy Spirit," but rather "let nothing be renewed except...that the hand is to be imposed upon him in penance." Thus Stephen not only does not advise iteration of Confirmation, but expressly forbids it by forbidding that anything of the baptismal rite be renewed, while at the same time he orders the imposition of hands for reconciliation.[30]

Thus, it is reconciliation with the church that Tertullian must intend when he refers to the blood of martyrdom as being not only able to effect baptism "when it has not been received" but also to "restore it [i.e., baptism] when lost." As has been seen, it is the sacrament of penance/reconciliation that normally restores the graced state of baptismal communion in the sacramental system of the Catholic church. Tertullian allows that the blood of martyrdom can effect not only baptism for the non-Christian who dies for Christ, but also sacramental reconciliation with the church by restoring the grace of baptismal communion lost through heresy or schism, or any other grave sin. Indeed, it is "Tertullian's idea that there is only one way that such [grave] sins committed after baptism can be forgiven: the baptism of blood.... This is because martyrdom is an *aliud baptisma...secunda regeneratio, secunda intinctio, secundum lavacrum*" [another baptism...a second birth, a second immersion, a second bath].[31] Consequently, martyrdom, here, has an effect analogous to sacramental reconciliation, restoring the grace of baptism without repeating the sacrament.[32]

MARTYRDOM AS "SUPRASACRAMENT"

In this context, it is timely to recall the fragment of the ancient father Melito of Sardis (†180) quoted earlier, that "two things constitute provision for the forgiveness of sins: suffering for Christ and baptism."[33] The fragment survives without its context, and has been received, as previously noted, as the earliest reference to baptism of blood. However, it seems reasonable to suggest that Melito may have had in mind not merely two species of baptism, but that his focus on "forgiveness of sins" implies that martyrdom is analogous not only to sacramental baptism but also to penance and reconciliation, by effecting forgiveness of sins for those already baptized.

Baptism of blood, however, was considered to effect the grace of baptism but not baptism's ecclesial consequence. In other words, baptism by blood gained salvation and conformity to the heavenly Christ, but not entry into his earthly Body, the church:

> Hence according to the ancient conviction of faith, martyrdom has not the ecclesiological effect of baptism, which means nothing to the martyr, since he is not to live in the realm where the Church exists as a sign of God's kingship on earth. But martyrdom does possess the grace effected by baptism, as conformity with Christ dying in sacrifice out of love of the Father.[34]

Unlike sacramental baptism by water, baptism by blood does not impart a sacramental character, only sacramental grace.[35] The sacramental character of baptism by water is "the indelible spiritual mark (*character*) of his belonging to Christ."[36] The sacramental character is ordered to the life of the earthly church militant, since "every baptised person is subject to the jurisdiction of the Church," including inculpable heretics and schismatics.[37] This character entitles the baptized to "receive the other sacraments... and to receive all the treasures of grace and truth, which Christ transmitted to His Church...and therefore imposes the obligation on the recipient to live a Christian mode of life."[38] Thus, the sacramental character of baptism by water is directly linked to the living of a Christian life in the earthly church:

> Incorporated into the Church by Baptism, the faithful have received the sacramental character that consecrates them for Christian religious worship. The baptismal seal enables and commits Christians to serve God by a vital participation in the holy liturgy of the Church and to exercise their baptismal priesthood by the witness of holy lives and practical charity.[39]

For the non-Christian who receives baptism by blood, living the Christian life in the church is not at issue, and so the sacramental character of baptism is not relevant. However, for the non-Catholic Christian, who has been obliged to live "a Christian mode of life" by virtue of the sacramental character of a valid baptism, and to do so "subject to the jurisdiction of the Church," the blood of martyrdom does have an ecclesial significance. As noted previously, the blood of "*martyria* unto death, [effects] the truest communion possible with Christ who shed his Blood, and by that sacrifice brings near those who once were far off" (*Ut Unum Sint* 84). The truest possible communion with Christ must involve communion with Christ's Body, the church, for the two cannot be separated. Seen from another perspective, martyrdom brings about a mode of communion with the Catholic church in its eucharistic worship, for "the martyr lives, and gives life, above all through his death, and thus he has himself entered into the eucharistic mystery."[40]

Martyrdom thus restores the inculpable non-Catholic Christian martyr to his proper condition within the church that was originally established by the sacramental character of his original baptism. While martyrdom as baptism of blood for the non-Christian has no ecclesial effect in terms of living in the earthly church,[41] martyrdom does have an ecclesial effect for the inculpable non-Catholic, as it restores the original relationship of the validly baptized to the church that lies in the sacramental character of baptism, and restores full eucharistic communion with the church because "the Christian who offers his life in martyrdom enters into full communion with the Pasch of Jesus Christ and thus becomes Eucharist with him" (*Sacramentum Caritatis* 85). In this sense, it clearly acts analogously not to baptism by blood but to penance and reconciliation by blood.

We can now appreciate Karl Rahner's judgment that while "martyrdom is not called a sacrament in the common sense of the word because it does not belong to the daily and normal order of the holy signs instituted by Christ," it is nevertheless "always something extraordinary":

That which had previously been signified and made present through the sacramental sign of Baptism is here simply fulfilled, namely dying and being baptised into the death of Christ. But even if we cannot call martyrdom a sacrament in the usual sense of the word, we refuse it this title, not because it is something less than a sacrament, but because it is something more....One could say that martyrdom is the only "supra-sacrament" which does not admit of an obstacle in the receiver, and in which the valid sacrament always and infallibly brings forth its fruit of eternal life.[42]

Therefore, it is proposed that the reconciliation by blood intrinsic to what Rahner calls the "supra-sacrament" of martyrdom is, in the case of inculpable non-Catholics killed in hatred of Christ, the engine supplying momentum to the ecumenism of blood. Far from being an innovation, reconciliation by blood has long been present, latent, unnamed, and undeveloped in Catholic doctrine, especially in recent papal teaching prior to that of Pope Francis.

5

Applying Reconciliation by Blood

IN THE Catholic tradition, blood spilled for Christ has the power to effect the grace of baptism for the unbaptized martyr. It is regarded as the seed of the church by which she grows despite the numerical losses of her martyrs. Yet the tradition allowed no value to the blood of the heretic and schismatic spilled for Christ. This view is still held with little reflection by many at the grassroots of the church.[1]

We have noted the fluidity in doctrine in the early church, with the result that many would actively choose one doctrine or theological faction over the orthodox one, which is the essence of heresy.[2] Such a choice led to that breach of communion the church called schism.[3] Such a deliberate choice of heterodoxy over orthodoxy, or of a local faction over and against the wider church was of its nature contumacious. Contumacy, as has been noted, is the stubborn refusal to obey or comply with authority.[4] However, the progress of time and the establishment and normalization of these breaches of communion, especially given the increasing practice of infant baptism,[5] meant that new members were being added to schismatic and heretical churches. These new members were not making a contumacious rejection of the Catholic church but were being initiated into the expression of Christianity that prevailed in their particular sociocultural context. From the perspective of the expanded ecclesial vision outlined here, it can be accepted that, in hindsight, they were not contumacious, and therefore inculpable of the state of schism that they had passively inherited, not actively chosen.

It was seen earlier that in modern Catholic canon law, the crimes of heresy and schism can now be applied only to those baptized or received directly into the Catholic church and who later make a free, deliberate, and obstinate—a contumacious—choice for heresy or schism. Those Christians who inherit schism by birth and baptism into those separated Christian communities are not in schism contumaciously, and so cannot be subject to the censure of excommunication reserved for contumacious schismatics. Indeed, recent magisterial teaching in the Catholic church affirms that such inculpably schismatic Christians are in a real, if imperfect, communion with the Catholic church, not least through their valid baptism that makes them de facto members of the Catholic church, however imperfect and incomplete their membership. Moreover, papal teaching has affirmed that such Christians who are killed in hatred of Christ undergo a martyrdom that perfects their communion with Christ and so with Christ's Body, the church. Nevertheless, this perfection of communion seems to be recognized only *coram Deo*, in the heavenly church rather than the earthly one.

THE CASE OF THE COPTS REVISITED

The highly publicized deaths of the twenty Copts and their Muslim companion in hatred of Christ by Daesh in February 2015, and Pope Francis's informal recognition of them as martyrs based on the principle of "ecumenism of blood," raises the question as to whether these twenty-one Coptic martyrs of Libya offer an opportunity to advance the reception of ecumenism of blood. Since the Catholic church can accept that—*coram Deo*, at least—inculpably schismatic martyrs can achieve perfect communion with Christ by the blood of their martyrdom, could the Catholic church now move forward to recognize formally this perfect communion *coram Ecclesia Catholica* in the case of these twenty-one martyrs?

In the face of increased persecution of Christians in situations where they are a relatively powerless minority, the restoration of Christian solidarity in the martyrs' blood is something that is arguably not only desirable, but necessary. The Libyan martyrs offer an ideal test case for the principle of reconciliation by blood that is implied in the ecumenism of blood. In this chapter, we will determine that on a doctrinal level there is no impediment to a formal recognition of these martyrs by the Catholic church. In the next chapter, we will discuss an existing ecclesial mechanism that could enable the formal recognition of the Libyan martyrs *coram Ecclesia Catholica*.

First, the status of the Coptic church regarding the Catholic church needs to be clarified. The Coptic church traces its foundation to the apostle Mark's ministry in the Egyptian city of Alexandria. Christians make up between 5 and 10 percent of the Egyptian population, and of them the overwhelming majority is Coptic.[6] The Coptic church, however, is not in communion with Rome due to the fifth-century Christological maelstrom of heresies that resulted from an attempt to understand more fully the identity of Christ.

At one extreme was Nestorianism,[7] which was pitted against another extreme, Eutychianism.[8] At the heart of the debate was confusion in the use of terms, with *prosopon*, *hypostasis*, *ousia*, and *physis* all being used by the various parties at various times to signify "person," "substance," "nature," or "being." Schism was inevitable given the heat surrounding the debates and the Machiavellian tactics often employed by the parties involved.[9] At the Council of Chalcedon in 451, what was intended as a definitive settlement was reached, involving a compromise that combined the views of Cyril of Alexandria and Pope Leo I of Rome.[10] Its definition employed some of these controverted words in a definite way:

> ...one and the same Christ, Son, Lord, Only-begotten, to be acknowledged in two natures [*duo physesin*], inconfusedly, unchangeably, indivisibly, inseparably; the distinction of natures being by no means taken away by the union, but rather the property of each nature being preserved, and concurring in one Person [*prosopon*] and one Subsistence [*hypostasin*], not parted or divided into two persons, but one and the same Son, and only begotten, God the Word, the Lord Jesus Christ.[11]

This dyophysite definition located the two distinct natures, human and divine, in one person and one basic reality. For the Alexandrians, this was too close to Nestorianism. Those who upheld the Chalcedonian formula saw the Alexandrian response as tantamount to Eutychianism's monophysite (*monos*, "alone," "one") teaching. However, many of those who rejected Chalcedon's definition also rejected Eutychianism, and saw themselves as miaphysite (*mia*, "one," "single"). The wounds of mutual recrimination ran deep, and with imperial politics adding to the confusion, the divisions were consolidated by the emergence of the Oriental Orthodox churches. In Egypt, the separateness of the Alexandrian church was entrenched by the support of the Roman Empire for the Chalcedonian settlement, the rise of Islam in the near east, and the continued use of Coptic rather than Greek in Alexandrian worship.[12]

In 1442, at the Council of Florence, the Catholic and Coptic churches formally declared their reunion. However, despite Rome's efforts, it was not carried into actual effect, apart from the short-lived reconciliation to Rome of the Coptic Patriarch of Alexandria (John XVI) in 1713.[13] In 1741, the Coptic bishop of Jerusalem was reconciled with Rome, and here lie the origins of the Coptic

Catholic church. The existence of this Uniate church to which the Coptic church is historically "intensely hostile"[14] is the only thorn in what are otherwise good relations between the Catholic and Coptic churches, with the latter having "no historical animus toward the Latin church or the Roman see, with which, indeed, the church of Alexandria has historically been allied."[15]

The ecumenical project approved by Vatican II has renewed Catholic efforts to heal the historic divisions among the churches. On a juridical level, a small bridge, admittedly conditional, of sacramental communion with the Eastern churches was established in the 1983 Code of Canon Law of the Roman Catholic church, which allows Catholics to receive the Eucharist, penance, and anointing of the sick from ministers of non-Catholic churches with valid sacraments, if it is "physically or morally impossible to approach a Catholic minister," while also allowing Catholic ministers to offer the same sacraments to members of "Eastern Churches which do not have full communion with the Catholic Church if they seek such of their own accord."[16]

REPAIRING CATHOLIC–COPTIC RELATIONS

There has been progress, too, at a theological level with the Coptic church. Following a series of consultations in Vienna from September 7 to 12, 1971, the Catholic and Coptic churches issued an agreed-upon formula of Christological belief:

> We believe that our Lord and Saviour, Jesus Christ, is God the Son Incarnate; perfect in his divinity and perfect in his humanity. His divinity was not separated from his humanity for a single moment, not for the twinkling of an eye. His humanity is one with his divinity without commixtion, without confusion, without division, without separation. We in our common faith

in the one Lord Jesus Christ, regard his mystery inexhaustible and ineffable and for the human mind never fully comprehendible or expressible.[17]

Based on this statement alone, an Oriental bishop from the Malankara Syrian Orthodox church in India, speaking from a theological tradition common to the Copts, was able to say,

> There is thus no doubt that the area of Christological agreement between the Roman Catholic Church and the Ancient Oriental Orthodox Church is vast and substantially complete. It is this agreement that gives us confidence to go ahead to look at the areas of disagreement in a genuine spirit of love and brotherhood. We do not need any longer to accuse each other of Eutychianism or Nestorianism or even of Monophysitism (understood as affirming only one nature) or of Diophysitism (if this means a separation of the united natures).[18]

Weeks later, the head of the Syrian Orthodox church (another non-Chalcedonian[19] Oriental church in communion with the Coptic church), Patriarch Mar Ignatius Jacob III of Antioch, met with Pope Paul VI in Rome. At the end of their private meeting, they issued a common declaration, which stated *inter alia,*

> The Pope and the Patriarch have recognized the deep spiritual communion, which already exists between their Churches. The celebration of the sacraments of the Lord, the common profession of faith in the Lord Jesus Christ, the Word of God made man for man's salvation, the apostolic traditions which form part of the common heritage of both Churches, the great Fathers and Doctors, including Saint Cyril of Alexandria, who are their common masters in the faith all these testify

to the action of the Holy Spirit who has continued to work in their Churches even when there have been human weakness and failings. The period of mutual recrimination and condemnation has given place to a willingness to meet together in sincere efforts to lighten and eventually remove the burden of history which still weighs heavily upon Christians.

Progress has already been made and Pope Paul VI and the Patriarch Mar Ignatius Jacob III are in agreement that there is no difference in the faith they profess concerning the mystery of the Word of God made flesh and become really man, even if over the centuries difficulties have arisen out of the different theological expressions by which this faith was expressed. They therefore encourage the clergy and faithful of their Churches to even greater endeavours at removing the obstacles which still prevent complete communion among them.[20]

The two leaders affirmed the basic elements of the imperfect but real communion between their two churches. Significant is the express acknowledgment of past difficulties, not least due to "different theological expressions," and the intention to move beyond them to "remove the burden of history...[and] the obstacles which still prevent complete communion." The declaration manifests a clear will to reestablish communion.

In 1973, further progress was made when Pope Paul VI welcomed the Coptic pope, Shenouda III, to the Vatican where they issued a common declaration of faith, which is detailed and comprehensive. In it, they recognize the context in which their ecumenical endeavors are pursued:

We humbly recognize that our Churches are not able to give more perfect witness to this new life in Christ because of existing divisions which have behind them centuries of difficult history. In fact, since the year 451

A.D., theological differences, nourished and widened by non-theological factors, have sprung up. These differences cannot be ignored. In spite of them, however, we are rediscovering ourselves as Churches with a common inheritance and are reaching out with determination and confidence in the Lord to achieve the fullness and perfection of that unity which is His gift.[21]

It has already been shown that an example of the "common inheritance" that the two churches share is the "communion... already perfect in what we all consider the highest point of the life of grace, *martyria* unto death" (*Ut Unum Sint* 84). Again, there is the acknowledgment of a burden of "difficult history" that is matched by a determination to achieve the "fullness and perfection" of communion. By this declaration, the Coptic church effectively confirms the Catholic–Syrian Orthodox joint declaration.

At the same meeting, the two popes established an international joint commission to facilitate theological dialogue between the Catholic and Coptic churches. In 1976, the commission issued a Christological declaration that, while not having the weight of a common declaration by the heads of the churches, is nevertheless significant in expressing the consensus of a body established by and acting for the leaders of the two churches.[22] After a detailed profession of faith in the nature of Christ, the declaration concludes,

> This is our faith in the mystery of the Incarnation of Our Lord Jesus Christ and the economy of our salvation. In this we all agree.[23]

In 1984, Paul VI's successor, John Paul II, and Mar Ignatius Jacob III's successor, Mar Ignatius Zakka I Iwas, issued their own common declaration:

> Their Holinesses Pope John Paul II and Patriarch Zakka I wish solemnly to widen the horizon of their

brotherhood and affirm herewith the terms of the deep spiritual communion which already unites them...and to advance in finding a wholly common ecclesial life.

First of all, Their Holinesses confess the faith of their two Churches, formulated by Nicene Council of 325 A.D. and generally known as "the Nicene Creed." The confusions and schisms that occurred between their Churches in the later centuries, they realize today, in no way affect or touch the substance of their faith, since these arose only because of differences in terminology and culture and in the various formulae adopted by different theological schools to express the same matter.

Accordingly, we find today no real basis for the sad divisions and schisms that subsequently arose between us concerning the doctrine of Incarnation.

In words and life we confess the true doctrine concerning Christ our Lord, notwithstanding the differences in interpretation of such a doctrine which arose at the time of the Council of Chalcedon.

Hence we wish to reaffirm solemnly our profession of common faith in the Incarnation of our Lord Jesus Christ, as Pope Paul VI and Patriarch Mar Ignatius Jacob III did in 1971...[and] we pledge ourselves solemnly to do all that in us lies to remove the last obstacles still hindering full communion.[24]

This declaration expresses a clear and substantial development in the rapprochement between the Oriental churches and the Catholic church. The previous elements of the renewed assessment of the cause of their separation are restated and affirmed: "confusions...differences in terminology and culture and the various formulae adopted by different theological schools to express the same matter." Yet the new relationship is expressed in even stronger terms: a "deep spiritual communion" already exists and they now seek "a wholly common ecclesial life" since there is "no real basis for the sad divisions and schisms." "In words and life" and despite previous "differences in interpretation," they share "the true doctrine concerning Jesus Christ" and commit themselves "solemnly to do all that in us lies to remove the last obstacles still hindering full communion." Any tentativeness has now disappeared and there is here an unambiguous commitment to restoring communion.

The Coptic ratification of this pan-Oriental rapprochement with the Catholic church came in 1988. After the first meeting of the second phase of the Catholic-Coptic international joint commission's work, it reported that "we are grateful to God that we are now able to sign a common formula expressing our official agreement on Christology which was already approved by the Holy Synod of the Coptic Orthodox Church on June 21, 1986." *The Brief Formula* states,

> We believe that our Lord, God and Savior Jesus Christ, the Incarnate-Logos is perfect in His Divinity and perfect in His Humanity. He made His Humanity one with His Divinity without mixture nor mingling, nor confusion. His Divinity was not separated from His Humanity even for a moment or twinkling of an eye.
>
> At the same time, we Anathematize the Doctrines of both Nestorius and Eutyches.[25]

While this common formula is far briefer than that in the 1976 common declaration, the significance of this formula lies in its having been ratified by the synod of the Coptic church, elevating the work of the commission to the status of the official position of the Coptic church.

The work of this international joint commission appears to have ceased after 1993,[26] and been subsumed into a wider dialogue between the Catholic church and seven churches of the Oriental communion centered on the *International Joint Commission for Theological Dialogue Between the Catholic Church and the Oriental Orthodox Churches*, which was established in 2003 as a vehicle for the Oriental churches to "engage in an official dialogue with the Catholic Church."[27] Since then the commission has reported annually on its progress, discussing topics of mutual concern, in particular, over several years, the nature and shape of ecclesial communion.[28]

In January 2015, the Catholic-Oriental joint commission issued the document referred to in chapter 1, "The Exercise of Communion in the Life of the Early Church and Its Implications for Our Search for Communion Today." It was noted that it gave considerable space to the role of martyrdom as a "unique sign" of ecclesial communion. Recognizing the common doctrinal inheritance in which martyrdom is seen as "baptism of blood," it comments that martyrdom "even appears more filled with grace than baptism."[29] This phrase is pregnant with possibility, particularly regarding our proposal that reconciliation by blood is analogous to sacramental reconciliation in restoring baptismal communion with the Catholic church. The door has been opened to a new stage in the ecumenism of blood, communion in the veneration of common martyrs not only from the early church, but also from the contemporary church, such as the Coptic martyrs of Libya.

The most recent report of the Catholic-Oriental joint commission, from February 2016, noted the presence of Armenian prelates at the liturgy in St. Peter's Basilica on April 12, 2015, during which Pope Francis proclaimed the Armenian St. Gregory of Narek a doctor of the Catholic church.[30] This significant event will be discussed in the next chapter. If the ecumenical atmosphere is accepting of the ecumenism of blood, then the mechanism of equivalent canonization, by which Pope Francis proclaimed formal Catholic recognition of the Armenian St. Gregory of Narek, is the ideal means by which to advance it.

6

Equivalent Canonization

LIKE ALL the ancient churches of Christianity, the Catholic church may recognize that a person who has died is a saint, upon which declaration the person is included in the "canon," or list, of recognized saints:

> By *canonizing* some of the faithful, i.e., by solemnly proclaiming that they practiced heroic virtue and lived in fidelity to God's grace, the Church recognizes the power of the Spirit of holiness within her and sustains the hope of believers by proposing the saints to them as models and intercessors. "The saints have always been the source and origin of renewal in the most difficult moments in the Church's history."[1]

The church can be described as the "communion of saints."[2] The use of the word *saint* in this context is grounded in the Pauline use of the word to designate baptized members of the Christian community.[3] Through the title "communion of saints," the church is understood to possess a unity not only among its members on earth, but that this unity is also with its members in heaven (see *Lumen Gentium* 50).

MAKING SAINTS

The original saints were the martyrs, whose remains were carefully collected as relics by which their heroic witness could be symbolized and remembered. Martyrs were considered reborn into eternal life at the moment of their death, and a martyr's feast day was kept originally as a *dies natalis*, a birthday.[4] They were recognized by popular acclaim, but, in time, confirmation of the martyr's following, or *cultus*, lay with the local bishop, who could authorize veneration of a martyr within his own jurisdiction.[5] This "canonization" was effected by the enrolling of the saint's name in martyrologies (official catalogues, or canons, of saints), which served to list those saints who could be honored in the church's liturgy.[6]

As martyrdom became less common, other exemplars of Christian witness were sought in those who had shown heroic virtue, having lived a "white" martyrdom.[7] They also were canonized by popular acclaim evidenced in the growth of a *cultus* around their memory. By the fifth century, the growing proliferation of saints led to the adoption of certain criteria, not always systematically applied, for recognizing a saint.[8] Between the fifth and tenth centuries, bishops took greater control over the recognition of new saints, and canonization was achieved by the "translation" of a saint's bones to an altar and the assigning of a feast day for the liturgical commemoration of the saint.[9]

The first martyrologies of saints were local or regional documents. The desire for more universal recognition of certain saints led to the first formal canonization—that of Ulrich of Augsburg in 993 by Pope John XV. This began an increasing systematization and centralization in the making of saints until the papacy took complete control in the seventeenth century.[10] The modern process of papal canonization has the feel of a criminal trial in which the candidate's life and virtues are examined in detail.[11] If approved, the name of the saint is enrolled by papal decree in the Catholic church's universal liturgical calendar. The current procedure was established by John Paul II in 1983.[12]

REVIVING AN ANCIENT WAY

There is, however, a second mechanism for canonization, which bypasses the current complex juridical procedure: equivalent canonization. First described in the eighteenth century by Prospero Lambertini (Pope Benedict XIV) in his work previously cited, *De Servorum Dei Beatificatione et Beatorum Canonizatione*, it occurs when a pope on his own authority decrees the addition of a saint's name to the liturgical calendar of the universal church, "omitting the judicial process and the ceremonies."[13]

In the last few years, this mechanism has been employed on several occasions. For example, on May 10, 2012, Pope Benedict XVI "extended the liturgical cult of St. Hildegard of Bingen (1089–1179) to the universal Church."[14] A few months later, on October 7, he further declared her a doctor of the church.[15]

Pope Francis has also made use of this mechanism. On October 11, 2013, he "extended the liturgical cult of Blessed Angela of Foligno (†1309) to the universal Church."[16] Two months later, he did the same for the first Jesuit priest, Blessed Peter Faber (†1546).[17] All these were Roman Catholics and were judged by the pope to have satisfied the three conditions listed by the Prefect of the Congregation for the Causes of Saints, Cardinal Angelo Amato: a long-standing *cultus*, historical agreement by experts on the candidate's virtues or martyrdom, and an uninterrupted reputation for wonders when invoked by the faithful.[18]

It is evident that the Coptic martyrs of Libya, having died less than two years ago, might be able to meet only the second of these conditions. However, such considerations are irrelevant in the case of those who have been canonized already by other churches. In such a case, the Catholic church could not attempt its own canonization of the saints in question; rather, it would acknowledge the canonization of the other church by adding that saint to the Catholic martyrology. This would have been largely hypothetical until February 21, 2015, when Pope Francis declared the Armenian Apostolic saint Gregory of Narek (†1005) the thirty-sixth doctor of the universal church.

AN ARMENIAN PRECEDENT

There was little published by way of explanation from the Vatican regarding this unexpected papal act. Vatican Radio offered a brief biography of him,[19] which did not address the significance of the crucial fact that during his life St. Gregory was a monk of a church not in communion with the Catholic church.

The Armenian Apostolic church is a non-Chalcedonian Oriental church like the Coptic church. It is also involved in the current dialogue with the Catholic church centered on the *International Joint Commission for Theological Dialogue between the Catholic Church and the Oriental Orthodox Churches.* Nor has it been a silent partner in this ecumenical rapprochement. In 1970, Paul VI and the Armenian Apostolic catholicos Vasken I issued a joint declaration in which they expressed a common will to "respond with greater fidelity to the call of the Holy Spirit stimulating them to a more profound unity."[20] In 1996, John Paul II and Karekin I, Vasken I's successor, issued their own common declaration, which expressed more strongly their shared ecumenical project, echoing the themes found in the joint statements with the Syrian and Coptic leaders—a real though imperfect communion that dispelled ancient misunderstandings and confusions, and a firm commitment to recovering full communion:

> Pope John Paul II and Catholicos Karekin I recognize the deep spiritual communion which already unites them and the Bishops, clergy and lay faithful of their Churches....Recent developments of ecumenical relations

and theological discussions carried out in the spirit of Christian love and fellowship have dispelled many misunderstandings inherited from the controversies and dissensions of the past....

The communion already existing between the two Churches and the hope for and commitment to recovery of full communion between them should become factors of motivation for further contact, more regular and substantial dialogue, leading to a greater degree of mutual understanding and recovery of the communality of their faith and service.[21]

Another cordial joint declaration followed on November 9, 2000, with Karekin I's successor, Karekin II.[22] The Armenian Apostolic church and the Coptic church have an equivalent status for the Catholic church, both being non-Chalcedonian Oriental churches in active dialogue with the Catholic church through their shared membership in the *International Joint Commission for Theological Dialogue between the Catholic Church and the Oriental Orthodox Churches*. Therefore, the Catholic declaration of the Armenian St. Gregory of Narek as a doctor of the church offers an apparent precedent for the formal recognition of the Coptic martyrs of Libya.

Yet it should be noted that St. Gregory of Narek was already recognized implicitly as a saint by the Roman church given that he was a saint not just of the Armenian Apostolic church, but also of its estranged uniate daughter, the Armenian Catholic church.

The Armenian church has perhaps an even more complicated history of relations with the Catholic church than the Coptic church. The portion of the Armenian Apostolic church that lay within the crusader states was reconciled with Rome for a time in the twelfth century, prompted as much by a shared dislike of the Greeks as anything else.[23] Benedict XIV (our friend Lambertini) accepted the reconciliation of an Armenian Apostolic prelate in Cilicia in 1742,[24] from which emerged the Armenian Catholic church, a year after the Coptic Catholic church was born.

Significantly, when this group of Armenians was reconciled to form the Armenian Catholic church, they brought with them St. Gregory of Narek and all their particular saints who had not been directly involved in causing the schism. While the feasts of these saints were celebrated only by the Armenian Catholics, the saints were effectively accepted by the Roman Catholic church as a result of the restoration of communion. This is the position of the uniate, or Eastern Catholic, churches:

> Schismatic saints are acceptable; saints who caused schisms are a contradiction in terms.[25]

It should be noted that neither the Coptic nor Armenian Catholic churches can now canonize new saints, as they are subject to the centralization of this power in the Roman papacy.[26]

Thus, the use of equivalent canonization for St. Gregory of Narek was not of the same nature as for the Catholics who had been canonized this way. St. Gregory was not canonized per se, but his name was inserted into the liturgical calendar (February 27) of the *Roman* Catholic church. Thus, it was not a canonization but merely the inclusion in the Roman Catholic liturgy of a saint shared by both an Oriental church and its Eastern Catholic counterpart. In doing so, it employed the mechanism of equivalent canonization: enrollment in the Roman liturgical calendar. Not only did this mechanism avoid encroaching on the prerogatives of another church, but it was also a profound gesture of communion and solidarity in the context of the commemoration of the centenary of the Armenian genocide.[27]

This ecumenical gesture was well received by the Armenian Apostolic church. After the Mass on April 12, 2015, Armenian Catholicos Karekin II delivered an address in which he expressed approval of St. Gregory's elevation to doctor of the universal church and accepted the ecumenism of blood:

> During this sacred service testifying to the friendship of Our two sister Churches, to the contentment of

Our people and to Us, one of Our Armenian Church Fathers—Saint Gregory of Narek—was declared by Your Holiness, per the designation of the Catholic Church, a "Doctor of the Church."...Dear Brother in Christ, We share Your view that martyrdom does not recognize the differences of denominations.[28]

In June 2016, Pope Francis visited Armenia at the invitation of Karekin II and the Armenian government. During a celebration of the Armenian liturgy, Karekin II reiterated in his homily the strengthened bonds between the two churches:

Dear ones, during these days together with our spiritual brother, Pope Francis, with joint visits and prayers we reconfirmed that the Holy Church of Christ is one in the spreading of the gospel of Christ in the world, in taking care of creation, standing against common problems, and in the vital mission of the salvation of man who is the crown and glory of God's creation.... On this graceful day we are appreciative for another opportunity to thank Pope Francis on the occasion of his brotherly visit. We and our people will always pray for you, beloved brother, and for your efforts made towards peace and prosperity of humanity and towards the advancement of the Church of Christ.[29]

At the conclusion of the same liturgy, Pope Francis responded,

May the Armenian Church walk in peace and may the communion between us be complete....On this holy Sunday may we follow God's call to full communion and hasten towards it.[30]

Later that day, the two leaders issued a joint declaration that recognized a new and enhanced relationship between the two churches:

We gladly confirm that despite continuing divisions among Christians, we have come to realize more clearly that what unites us is much more than what divides us. This is the solid basis upon which the unity of Christ's Church will be made manifest, in accordance with the Lord's words, "that they all may be one." Over the past decades the relationship between the Armenian Apostolic Church and the Catholic Church has successfully entered a new phase, strengthened by our mutual prayers and joint efforts in overcoming contemporary challenges. Today we are convinced of the crucial importance of furthering this relationship, engaging in deeper and more decisive collaboration not only in the area of theology, but also in prayer and active cooperation on the level of the local communities, with a view to sharing full communion and concrete expressions of unity.[31]

THE COPTIC MARTYRS OF LIBYA

The declaration of St. Gregory of Narek as a doctor of the Catholic church has contributed significantly to the deepening of communion between the Catholic and Armenian Apostolic churches. Given, as outlined earlier, the equally positive relationship between the Catholic and Coptic churches, the time seems ripe for the Catholic church to make a gesture of similar magnanimity to the Copts by inserting into the Catholic liturgical calendar the names of the Libyan martyrs canonized by the Coptic church in February 2015.

As with the Armenian St. Gregory of Narek, any formal Catholic recognition of the Coptic martyrs of Libya could be achieved without violating the prerogatives of another church. In the first place, the Coptic church has already canonized the twenty-one martyrs of Libya. The Coptic process for canonization is the simple act of insertion into its liturgical calendar by the patriarch, and on February 21, 2015, the Coptic Pope Tawadros II decreed that the Libyan martyrs' feast would be kept on February 15 (that date as reckoned in the Gregorian calendar).[32] Considering the recent precedents of equivalent canonization detailed previously, it is reasonable to suggest that Pope Francis could extend the liturgical commemoration of the Coptic martyrs of Libya to the Catholic church by inserting their feast into the Roman liturgical calendar.

The Coptic Catholic church could present a potential obstacle since relations between it and the Coptic church, as noted earlier, are not as warm as those between the Roman Catholic church and the Coptic Orthodox. However, there are signs that this need not be a disincentive. In the days following the deaths of the twenty-one martyrs of Libya, the Coptic Catholic bishop of Sohag in Egypt acknowledged the Libyan martyrs as genuine martyrs:

> The Church in Egypt has been strengthened by the murder of our brothers in Libya....They suffered a holy death with prayers on their lips. They went to their deaths just like the early Christians.[33]

A month later, another Coptic Catholic bishop in Egypt, Kyrillos Samaan of Assiut, offered a similar recognition of the Coptic martyrs during an interview, following the lead taken by Pope Francis:

> The Coptic Orthodox Church has already recognized these 21 murdered Christians as martyrs and included them in their calendar of the Saints. Do Catholics also regard them as martyrs? "Yes, undoubtedly," says Bishop Kyrillos William Samaan, the Coptic Catholic Bishop of Assiut in Upper Egypt. "Pope Francis himself said that, after their murder. He recognized them as martyrs. They were killed because they were Christians. Their killers were hunting for Christians in order

to abduct them. The victims were full of faith right up to the end. They remained faithful to Jesus. Their last words were words like: 'Lord Jesus, have mercy!' And so they are true martyrs—for us Catholics as well."[34]

Given the positive attitude to the Libyan martyrs by the Coptic Catholic church, formal recognition of the Coptic martyrs of Libya by their insertion into the liturgical calendar of the Roman church should provoke no negative reaction from Coptic Catholics. Moreover, given the positive response of the Armenian Apostolic church to Pope Francis's declaration of St. Gregory of Narek as a doctor of the Catholic church, and the strengthened communion that resulted, the signs are very positive that the Coptic Orthodox church would be as equally welcoming of a similar gesture.

In May 2016, Pope Francis reemphasized the positive relationship between the Catholic and Coptic churches in a pontifical letter to Pope Tawadros II of Alexandria:

I express my joy at the ever-deeper spiritual bonds uniting the See of Peter and the See of Mark.

It is with gratitude to the Lord our God that I recall the steps we have taken together along the path of reconciliation and friendship. After centuries of silence, misunderstanding and even hostility, Catholics and Copts increasingly are encountering one another, entering into dialogue, and cooperating together in proclaiming the Gospel and serving humanity. In this renewed spirit of friendship, the Lord helps us to see that the bond uniting us is born of the same call and mission we received from the Father on the day of our baptism. Indeed, it is through baptism that we become members of the one Body of Christ that is the Church (cf. 1 Cor 12:13), God's own people, who proclaim his praises (cf. 1 Pet 2:9). May the Holy Spirit, the mainspring and bearer of all gifts, unite us evermore in the bond of Christian love and guide us in our shared pilgrimage, in truth and charity, towards full communion.[35]

The equivalent canonization of the Coptic martyrs of Libya, given recent precedents and building on an ever-strengthening ecumenical rapprochement, would be a fitting testament to the bond uniting the Catholic and Coptic churches in their common baptism by also confirming their unity in the blood of martyrs.

7

Conclusion

IN OUR consideration of the Coptic martyrs of Libya in light of Pope Francis's bold advocacy of the ecumenism of blood, we have addressed two questions: *Can the principle of ecumenism of blood be reconciled with Catholic doctrine* and *can the Catholic church formally recognize the Coptic Orthodox church's canonization of the twenty-one martyrs of Libya?*

IS ECUMENISM OF BLOOD CATHOLIC?

Regarding the first question, we have argued that the ecumenism of blood *is* able to be reconciled with Catholic doctrine. The high value placed on martyrdom for Christ throughout the Catholic tradition is such that it is regarded as baptizing the unbaptized martyr, with blood replacing water. For the baptized, as the act of perfect discipleship, martyrdom absolves serious postbaptismal sin. For heretics and schismatics, however, patristic and conciliar teaching denied any benefit from martyrdom. From the eighteenth century, a more nuanced view emerged, with

Prospero Lambertini recognizing the possibility of an invincible heretic of good faith, one who has not contumaciously chosen separation from the Catholic church but inherited it or has suffered from an inadequate preaching of Catholic teaching. Such an invincible heretic could be a true martyr *coram Deo*, though not *coram Ecclesia*.

The development of that teaching to Vatican II and beyond allows us to identify the category of inculpable schismatic, by analogy with the inculpable ignorance advanced by Stephen Bullivant. This inculpability is recognized effectively in the canon law of the Catholic church, which now assumes the inculpability of those who belong in good faith to churches not in communion with Rome. At first glance, this exempts them from the Catholic church's traditional refusal to recognize authentic martyrdom of heretics and schismatics killed in persecution. Moreover, insofar as they died for Christ, it is proposed that non-Catholic Christians can be accepted as martyrs in Catholic terms because, in a manner analogous to sacramental reconciliation, the blood of their martyrdom reconciles them to communion with the Catholic church as the inevitable fruit of the perfect conformity to Christ that the "supra-sacrament" of martyrdom achieves. In other words, they have been reconciled by their blood, just as unbaptized martyrs enter communion with the church having been baptized by their blood, and indeed in their self-sacrifice they "become Eucharist" with Christ.

Furthermore, recent ecumenical developments between the Catholic and the Coptic Orthodox and other Oriental churches have effectively negated the mutual accusations of heresy of previous centuries. Joint statements issued by the heads of the respective churches in recent decades affirm a common faith in such controverted areas as Christology. Recent papal and conciliar teaching has fostered the trend to contextualize disunity and affirmed a real if partial communion between the various churches through baptism, and through other elements, not least the witness of martyrs. Indeed, St. John Paul II was able to conclude that martyrdom for Christ brings with it perfect communion with the Catholic church.

I have explored the canonical and doctrinal resolution of the obstacle posed by heresy from the Catholic perspective, alongside an expanded understanding in Catholic doctrine of the general inculpability of members of separated churches in the matter of schism, and the recognition in papal teaching of the power of martyrs' blood to reconcile an individual into perfect communion with the Catholic church. Consequently, the ecumenism of blood, as a communion in martyrdom, may be considered consistent with Catholic teaching, and furthermore, is a legitimate development of recent papal and conciliar teaching.

CAN CATHOLICS CELEBRATE THE COPTIC MARTYRS?

Regarding the second question of whether the ecumenism of blood might allow the Catholic church to recognize in a formal way the Coptic canonization of its Libyan martyrs, an equally positive conclusion has been reached. The current ecclesiastical context is one of ever-strengthening rapprochement between the Catholic church and the Coptic Orthodox and other Oriental churches that has taken place over recent decades, with repeated and explicit commitments to restoring full communion from the leaders of the churches. Doctrinally, both the Catholic recognition of partial communion between the churches and John Paul II's clear teaching that martyrdom brings about the perfection of communion with Christ and his Body, the church, allow for the recognition of the martyrs of other churches *coram Ecclesia Catholica*. Pope Francis affirms this by his insistence that all martyrs constitute a common Christian patrimony.

On an ecclesial level, the formal recognition of the Coptic martyrs is clearly possible and even desirable. The recent history of the Oriental churches in increasingly hostile sociopolitical environments, and the ecumenical project to which the Catholic church has committed itself, make Catholic-Oriental solidarity attractive on both sides. A practical instrument to achieve this is found in the mechanism of equivalent canonization, the papal insertion of saints' names into the liturgical calendar of the Catholic church. Used several times in recent years for Catholic saints, this mechanism has also been applied very recently to an Oriental saint, the Armenian Apostolic St. Gregory of Narek. This has enabled the liturgical veneration of another church's canonized saint to be extended to the Catholic church without usurping the prerogatives of the other church. Significantly, this gesture was well-received by the Armenian Apostolic church.

While St. Gregory of Narek already had a foot in the Catholic door, as it were, through his status as a saint in the uniate Armenian Catholic church, the mechanism of insertion into the Roman calendar extended his *cultus* to the rest of the Catholic church. The uniate Coptic Catholic church has already informally recognized the Libyan martyrs, allowing the Roman Catholic church to grant them the same status as St. Gregory of Narek. Consequently, it lies within Pope Francis's authority to do for the Coptic martyrs of Libya what he did for the Armenian Apostolic St. Gregory of Narek: insert their names into the liturgical calendar of the Catholic church, thereby formally recognizing them as martyrs *coram Ecclesia Catholica*. Thus, in answer to our second question, it would be possible for the Catholic church to recognize formally and liturgically the Coptic martyrs of Libya by means of equivalent canonization. This would be a concrete manifestation of the ecumenism of blood.

ECUMENICAL IMPLICATIONS

Not only is it possible, formal Catholic recognition of the Coptic martyrs of Libya is also desirable. The edifice erected by centuries of mutual suspicion and recrimination has been increasingly eroded by the ecumenical engagement initiated by Vatican II. Pope Francis's insertion into the Catholic liturgical calendar of the Armenian Apostolic St. Gregory of Narek by declaring him a doctor of the Catholic church in 2015—at a time when the Armenian church was commemorating the hundredth anniversary of the Armenian genocide—led to Pope Francis being welcomed at the residence of the Armenian catholicos during the papal visit to Armenia in 2016. It is in gestures such as these that practical ecumenism is realized.

Just as timely was the common declaration of Popes Francis and Tawadros II on April 28, 2017. Here, the Catholic and Coptic popes looked back with fond memory on the earliest centuries of the Christian church:

> The full communion...existed between our churches... expressed through prayer and similar liturgical practices, the veneration of the same martyrs and saints, and in the development and spread of monasticism....This common experience of communion before the time of separation has a special significance in our efforts to restore full communion today....[and] challenge[s] us to intensify our common efforts to persevere in the search for visible unity in diversity, under the guidance of the Holy Spirit.[1]

In this declaration, the popes recalled their former communion in ancient times as an incentive to restore communion today, not least by decreeing that both churches "will seek sincerely not to repeat the baptism that has been administered in either of our Churches for any person who wishes to join the other."[2] The Coptic practice of rebaptizing Catholics seeking to enter the Coptic church had been the enduring thorn in the side of ecumenical progress between the two churches. By this mutual commitment not to rebaptize members of either church seeking to enter the other (for the sake of marriage, for example), each church now recognizes fully and formally the baptism administered by the other.

The removal of this obstacle to fraternity and communion seals the mutual regard the two churches now have for each other and the mutual desire for reestablishing the full communion of the first Christian centuries. Catholic liturgical celebration of the Coptic martyrs of Libya would be another concrete gesture of mutual regard, another step toward restoring full communion, through "the veneration of the same martyrs and saints."[3]

It is hoped that formal Catholic recognition of the Coptic martyrs would be desirable from a Coptic point of view as an act of solidarity in their time of need as well as a further step toward the full communion both churches desire. It is certainly desirable from a Catholic perspective as it would legitimately advance the ecumenical project to which the Catholic church is committed.

A further question remains, which is beyond the scope of this book but arises inevitably from it. It is one thing that the blood of the martyrs of ancient churches can restore their communion with the Catholic church—these churches were once in communion, their differences are increasingly being eroded by goodwill and the recognition of misunderstanding, and they share an apostolic ministry and sacramental life. What, then, of those newer Christian communities born of the Protestant Reformation? Their doctrinal differences are far greater, their ministry is often non-apostolic, and their sacramental life less developed.

Can the Catholic church similarly recognize as restored to its communion those Protestants who are martyred in hatred of Christ? Developments since Pope Paul VI canonized the martyrs of Uganda and the trajectory of the argument discussed in proposing reconciliation by blood suggest the viability of this question. After all, we can already say of any Christian that "this communion is already perfect in what we all consider the highest point of the life of grace, *martyria* unto death, the truest communion possible with Christ who shed his Blood, and by that sacrifice brings near those who once were far off" (*Ut Unum Sint* 84).

Epilogue

A DEVELOPMENT OF UNDERSTANDING

HAVING REACHED this point, there emerge two lingering questions. First, and most swiftly addressed, is whether reconciliation by blood, as proposed here, represents a change in Catholic doctrine regarding heresy and schism. I have sought to show that it represents a legitimate development of Catholic doctrine, not a change in it. For example, consider the church's teaching on suicide.

In absolute terms, suicide is gravely sinful in Catholic teaching. What has changed is that the church has used advances in medical science to comprehend that many, if not most, suicides are of people in grave mental distress. In such distress, a person would be neither fully responsible nor free in moral terms for the act of suicide. In this case, though the act remains gravely sinful, the guilt of the person committing it is substantially mitigated. The Catholic church has therefore developed a framework for assessing individual cases in their proper and relevant context.

Similarly, the Catholic teaching on heresy and schism, and the gravity of these sins, remains intact in the principle of reconciliation by blood as outlined here. What has developed is the understanding of the context of individuals separated from the Catholic church by inherited schism. They are personally inculpable of this sin, a fact recognized formally in Catholic canon law. Thus, they are open to reconciliation with the Catholic church by the blood of their martyrdom as would any Catholic martyr who dies with sin still unabsolved. This fact can be formally and liturgically recognized. I am not suggesting that those who contumaciously and with full freedom and knowledge separate themselves from communion with the Catholic church can be absolved by martyr blood. The Catholic doctrinal tradition seems clear on that.

Second, if martyr blood can reconcile Copts, and other Oriental Christians, to the Catholic church, can it not do the same for the Orthodox and for Protestants? It is a logical and inescapable question that is beyond the scope of this work.

Our primary intention, here, has been to establish whether the principle of reconciliation by blood played an authentic role in the emerging ecumenism of blood. It did so by taking the best-case scenario that inspired it: martyrs of a church that has been long separated from the Catholic church but could no longer be doctrinally opposed to it. The enduring schism is now based only on the enduring legacy of history and human frailty. The Christological controversies that caused the breach have been resolved. Catholic liturgical recognition and co-celebration of the Coptic martyrs has been proposed as a justifiable gesture that might go some way to overcoming this very human, and thus very expendable, legacy.

ECUMENICAL QUESTIONS

But what of those Christian communities that are still theologically committed to opposing—to a greater or lesser extent—Catholic teaching? What of those Christian groups that disagree with the Catholic church about the procession of the Holy Spirit, or the sacramental economy, or the nature of the Mass? Can their members who are martyred for faith in Christ be likewise considered as reconciled to the one Body of Christ?

St. John Paul II may have such in mind in *Ut Unum Sint*, recognizing that such martyrs can be considered as having entered perfect communion with Christ, and so with the Body of Christ. This we can do with confidence if we employ Benedict XIV's distinction between *coram Deo* and *coram Eccelsia*—in the sight of God and in the sight of the church. St. John Paul II affirmed their perfect communion with the Body of Christ *coram Deo*. Since the Body of Christ cannot be split, non-Catholic martyrs in heaven must be in perfect communion with the church on earth.

It is the recognition on earth, *coram Ecclesia Catholica*, of their perfect heavenly communion that is the vexed issue. An elephant in the room is ecclesiastical imperialism. On this issue, I have sought to avoid any appearance of an unwanted encroachment by the Catholic church on the rights of another Christian community. What has been proposed, rather, is not Catholic canonization of the Coptic martyrs of Libya, but Catholic formal, liturgical recognition of their canonization by the Coptic church. Such a liturgical co-celebration is a real ecumenical advance that does not touch the identity and integrity of either church, but it builds a new bridge between them and adds impetus to our human efforts at reestablishing communion.

However, many Christian communities do not have a formal mechanism for canonizing saints. Some Protestant communities would balk at the very idea of the veneration of saints, let alone establishing a formal means to canonize them. While the Catholic church could recognize the martyrs from such communities as having entered perfect communion with the Body of Christ in heaven, *coram Deo*, it is powerless to recognize them on earth, *coram Ecclesia*, at the very least because their own communities would not canonize them. It would be indelicate, to say the least, for the Catholic church to canonize them despite their own communities. This is quite apart from the serious and often inescapable differences in doctrine between many of these communities and the Catholic church. It is for theologians of greater competence to determine any viable way forward.

For all that, one thing should be remembered. Every Christian church and community has its heroes, recognizing in its forbears those who stood valiantly for Christ in faith even to the point of death. Most would recognize past members who lived lives of heroic virtue, of true and Christ-like charity. In this, we hear echoes of the popular acclamation by which saints were first made in the church, since its very origins. Whether this provides a starting point for further discussion is up to those competent theologians invoked earlier. Nevertheless, it is a basic human need, and a Christian one too, to recognize heroes in the pursuit of an ideal, to honor their memory, and to cherish their example. Catholics, as do Eastern Christians and many Anglicans, see in such heroes not only models to emulate but confreres who have attained to the church of heaven, where they can pray for us at the throne of God more effectively than we on earth can pray for ourselves.

This treasure of the Communion of Saints is yet to be fully embraced by many non-Catholic Christians. Perhaps it is time they did, but that is for them to determine. This book offers a step toward an expansion in the Catholic vision of the Communion of Saints, one that has long been rich and inspiring. As the Communion of Saints has inspired countless Christians to persevere in faith, hope, and charity, so too might it now inspire all Christians to seek to fulfill Christ's desire that his disciples should be as one.

Notes

1. *Daesh* is the Arabic acronym for Islamic State in Iraq and al-Sham. In its Arabic context, it is undignified, and for that reason is greatly disliked by the group itself. See, for example, Rose Troup Buchanan, "Daesh: What Does the Word Mean? Is David Cameron's Use of It Significant?" *The Independent* (UK), December 2, 2015, http://www.independent.co.uk/news/uk/politics/daesh-isis-cameron-syria-air-strikes-a6757241.html. Hereafter, it will be the preferred name for the group.

2. *Open Doors World Watch List 2017*, accessed March 27, 2018, https://www.opendoorsusa.org/christian-persecution/world-watch-list/.

3. Ewelina Ochab, "Genocide in the Middle East," *ADF International Executive Summary Report*, May 12, 2016, no. 12, https://adflegal.blob.core.windows.net/international-content/docs/default-source/default-document-library/resources/campaign-resources/europe/middle-east---genocide/2016-05-19-memo-on-genocide-and-possible-steps-at-the-un-sc.pdf.

4. U.S. State Department, "Egypt," *International Religious Freedom Report for 2015*, accessed March 27, 2018, http://www.state.gov/j/drl/rls/irf/religiousfreedom/index.htm?year=2015&dlid=256263.

5. Center for the Study of Global Christianity, "Martyrdom Situations 2000–2010," July 2014, http://www.gordonconwell.edu/ockenga/research/documents/1martyrdomsituations.pdf.

6. Samuel Smith, "90,000 Christians Killed in 2016, 1 Every 6 Minutes: Study," *Christian Post*, December 30, 2016, https://www.christianpost.com/news/90000-christians-killed-in-2016-1-every-6-minutes-study-172464/.

7. Smith, "90,000 Christians Killed in 2016."

8. Center for the Study of Global Christianity, "Global Diagram 16: Evangelization through Martyrdom, 2001," accessed March 27, 2018, http://www.gordonconwell.edu/ockenga/research/documents/gd16.pdf.

9. Center for the Study of Global Christianity, "Status of Global Christianity, 2017, in the Context of 1900–2050," accessed March 27, 2018, http://www.gordonconwell.edu/ockenga/research/documents/StatusofGlobalChristianity2017.pdf.

10. Center for the Study of Global Christianity, "Status of Global Christianity."

11. Patrick Manning, "African Population, 1650–1950: Methods for New Estimates by Region," paper delivered at the *African Economic History Conference*, Vancouver, April 2013, 7, http://mortenjerven.com/wp-content/uploads/2013/04/AfricanPopulation.Methods.pdf.

12. Center for the Study of Global Christianity, "Status of Global Christianity."

13. United Nations, Department of Economic and Social Affairs, "Population Division, World Population Prospects: The 2015 Revision," accessed March 27, 2018, http://www.worldometers.info/world-population/africa-population/.

14. Rondo Cameron, *Concise Economic History of the World* (New York: OUP, 1993), 193.

15. Center for the Study of Global Christianity, "Status of Global Christianity."

16. United Nations, "World Population Prospects."

17. Center for the Study of Global Christianity, "Status of Global Christianity."

18. Various sources compiled at https://en.wikipedia.org/wiki/Church_attendance (accessed March 27, 2018).

19. Tertullian, *Apologeticus pro Christianis*, 50, in *The Ante-Nicene Fathers*, vol. 3, eds. Alexander Roberts, James Donaldson, and A. Cleveland Coxe (Buffalo: Christian Literature Publishing Co., 1885). See http://www.newadvent.org/fathers/0301.htm.

20. Elizabeth Scalia, "Witnesses to Martyrdom: Father Hamel's Last Moments," *Aleteia*, October 4, 2016, http://aleteia.org/2016/10/04/witnesses-to-martyrdom-father-hamels-last-moments/.

INTRODUCTION

1. *Vatican Radio*, "Coptic Church Recognizes Martyrdom of 21 Coptic Christians," February 21, 2015, https://zenit.org/articles/martyrdom-of-21-egyptian-coptic-christians-recognized-by-coptic-church/.

2. Some typical examples: Oliver Maksan, "First Fruits of 21 Copts' Martyrdom," March 24, 2015, https://zenit.org/articles/first-fruits-of-21-copts-martyrdom/; Andrea Gagliarducci, "Remember the Copts ISIS Martyred in Libya? This Priest Does," July 19, 2016, http://www.catholicnewsagency.com/news/remember-the-copts-isis-martyred-in-libya-this-priest-does-68914/; and Hugh Somerville-Knapman, "Can Catholics Recognise the 21 Murdered Coptic Christians as Martyrs?" February 24, 2015, https://disqus.com/home/discussion/cherald/can_catholics_recognise_the_21_murdered_coptic_christians_as_martyrs/.

3. For example, in an interview in *La Stampa* on December 14, 2013; a speech to the Armenian church on May 8, 2014; addresses on October 31, 2014, November 30, 2014, February 16, 2015, and July 3, 2015, *inter alia*. These and other examples will be discussed in detail later.

4. Some of the less impassioned objections include Laurence England, "They Didn't Die for Ecumenism," February

16, 2015, http://thatthebonesyouhavecrushedmaythrill.blogspot
.co.uk/2015/02/they-didnt-die-for-ecumenism.html; and Elliot
Milco, "Can Non-Catholics Be Martyrs?" February 18, 2015,
https://thejosias.com/2015/02/18/dubium-can-non-catholics
-be-martyrs//.

5. "The restoration of unity among all Christians is one
of the principal concerns of the Second Vatican Council." Second Vatican Council, *Unitatis Redintegratio* (Decree on Ecumenism), Rome, 1964, no. 1. See http://www.vatican.va/archive/
hist_councils/ii_vatican_council/documents/vat-ii_decree
_19641121_unitatis-redintegratio_en.html.

6. Cf. Tertullian, *Apologeticus pro Christianis*, 50.

7. *Catechism of the Catholic Church* (New York: Doubleday,
1995), no. 114 (hereafter, *CCC*).

8. Alberto Strumia, "Analogy," *Interdisciplinary Encyclopedia of Religion and Science*, 2010, III, 4. DOI: 10.17421/
2037-2329-2010-AS-1: http://inters.org/analogy.

9. Leo Scheffzyck, "Analogy of Faith," in *Sacramentum
Mundi*, ed. Karl Rahner, vol. 1 (London: Burns & Oates, 1968).

10. Hereafter, "Coptic church" will be generally, though not
exclusively, used as synonymous with "Coptic Orthodox church."

1. UNDERSTANDING THE ECUMENISM OF BLOOD

1. Andrea Tornielli, "Never Be Afraid of Tenderness," *La
Stampa: Vatican Insider*, December 14, 2013, http://www.lastampa
.it/2013/12/14/esteri/vatican-insider/en/never-be-afraid-of
-tenderness-5BqUfVs9r7W1CJIMuHqNeI/pagina.html.

2. "Address of Pope Francis to His Holiness Karekin
II, Supreme Patriarch and Catholicos of all Armenians with
his Entourage," May 8, 2014, http://w2.vatican.va/content/
francesco/en/speeches/2014/may/documents/papa-francesco
_20140508_patriarca-armeni.html.

3. "Address of His Holiness Pope Francis to Members of the Catholic Fraternity of Charismatic Covenant Communities and Fellowships," October 31, 2014, http://w2.vatican.va/content/francesco/en/speeches/2014/october/documents/papa-francesco_20141031_catholic-fraternity.html.

4. "Joint Declaration of Pope Francis and Ecumenical Patriarch Bartholomew I," November 30, 2014, https://www.patriarchate.org/-/joint-declaration-of-his-holiness-pope-francis-and-his-all-holiness-ecumenical-patriarch-bartholomew-november-30-2014-.

5. "Address of the Ecumenical Patriarch Bartholomew I to Pope Francis," November 30, 2014, https://www.patriarchate.org/-/address-by-his-all-holiness-ecumenical-patriarch-bartholomew-to-his-holiness-pope-francis-during-the-divine-liturgy-for-the-feast-of-st-andrew-in-the-. Here, there is the assumption that the adverb "regrettably" is directed not to the growth of unity but to the means enabling it.

6. "Homily of His Holiness Pope Francis at the Celebration of Vespers on the Solemnity of the Conversion of Saint Paul the Apostle," January 25, 2015, http://w2.vatican.va/content/francesco/en/homilies/2015/documents/papa-francesco_20150125_vespri-conversione-san-paolo.html.

7. Jared Malsin, "Christians Mourn Their Relatives Beheaded by ISIS," *Time*, February 23, 2015, http://time.com/3718470/isis-copts-egypt/. The twenty-first victim was identified as a Ghanaian Muslim, Mathew Ayairga, who professed a conversion to Christianity on camera in response to the faith of the other victims ("Their God is my God"), and so was murdered with them. See Stefan J. Bos, "African Man Turns to Christ Moments before Beheading," BosNewsLife.com, April 23, 2015, http://www.bosnewslife.com/35141-african-man-turns-to-christ-moments-before-beheading/.

8. "Address of His Holiness Pope Francis to the Moderator and Representatives of the Church of Scotland," February 16, 2015, http://w2.vatican.va/content/francesco/en/speeches/2015/

february/documents/papa-francesco_20150216_moderatore
-chiesa-scozia.html.

9. "Message of his Holiness Pope Francis to His Holiness
Abuna Matthias Patriarch of the Ethiopian Tewahedo Orthodox Church," April 20, 2015, http://w2.vatican.va/content/
francesco/en/messages/pont-messages/2015/documents/papa
-francesco_20150420_messaggio-abuna-matthias.html.

10. "Message of His Holiness Pope Francis to His Holiness
Tawadros II Pope of Alexandria and Patriarch of the See of Saint
Mark," May 10, 2015, http://w2.vatican.va/content/francesco/
en/messages/pont-messages/2015/documents/papa-francesco
_20150510_messaggio-tawadros-ii.html.

11. International Joint Commission for Theological Dialogue between the Catholic Church and the Oriental Orthodox Churches, "The Exercise of Communion in the Life of the
Early Church and Its Implications for Our Search for Communion Today," May 13, 2015, http://www.vatican.va/roman
_curia/pontifical_councils/chrstuni/anc-orient-ch-docs/rc_pc
_chrstuni_doc_20150513_exercise-communion_en.html.

12. Cyprian of Carthage, "Epistle 72: To Jubianus, Concerning the Baptism of Heretics," in Alexander Roberts, James Donaldson, and A. Cleveland Coxe, *The Ante-Nicene Fathers*, vol. 5
(Buffalo: Christian Literature Publishing Company, 1886), no.
21, http://www.newadvent.org/fathers/050672.htm.

13. International Joint Commission between the Catholic
Church and the Coptic Orthodox Church, *Common Report and
Brief Formula*, February 12, 1988, http://www.prounione.urbe
.it/dia-int/oo-rc_copt/doc/e_oo-rc_copt_1988.html.

14. See "Common Declaration of Pope Paul VI and the Pope
of Alexandria Shenouda III," May 10, 1973, http://www.vatican.va/
roman_curia/pontifical_councils/chrstuni/anc-orient-ch-docs/rc
_pc_christuni_doc_19730510_copti_en.html. Note: *Schism* is defined
in Roman Catholic canon law with reference to the papacy: "Schism
is the refusal of submission to the Supreme Pontiff or of communion with the members of the Church subject to him." Canon no.

751, *Code of Canon Law (Codex Iuris Canonici)* (Vatican City: Libreria Editrice Vaticana, 1983), (hereafter, *CIC*).

15. "The Exercise of Communion," no. 72.

16. "The Exercise of Communion," no. 73.

17. "Address of His Holiness Pope Francis to the Renewal in the Holy Spirit Movement," St. Peter's Square, July 3, 2015, http://w2 .vatican.va/content/francesco/en/speeches/2015/july/documents/ papa-francesco_20150703_movimento-rinnovamento-spirito .html.

18. Paul VI, *Homilia in Sollemni Canonizatione Beatorum: Caroli Lwanga, Matthiae Mulumba Kalemba et viginti sociorum Martyrum Ugandensium*, October 18, 1964, http://w2.vatican.va/content/ paul-vi/la/homilies/1964/documents/hf_p-vi_hom_19641018 _martiri-uganda.html. This homily will be referred to in greater detail later.

19. Tornielli, "Never Be Afraid of Tenderness."

20. Their story can be followed at a website dedicated to their memory. See http://www.luebeckermaertyrer.de/en/ (accessed March 28, 2017).

21. Manfred Plate, "Ihr Blut floß ineinander. Den vier Lübecker Blutzeugen zum Gedächtnis," *Christ in der Gegenwart*, 2/1994 (Freiburg: Verlag Herder, 1994).

22. Benedict XVI, "Address of His Holiness Benedict XVI to H.E. Mr Walter Jürgen Schmid, New Ambassador of the Federal Republic of Germany to the Holy See," September 13, 2010, http:// w2.vatican.va/content/benedict-xvi/en/speeches/2010/september/ documents/hf_ben-xvi_spe_20100913_amb-germania.html.

2. THE CATHOLIC DOCTRINE OF MARTYRDOM

1. "Martyrdom," in *The New Dictionary of Theology*, eds. Joseph Komonchak, Mary Collins, and Dermot Lane (Wilmington, DE: Michael Glazier, 1987), 629.

2. Komonchak et al., "Martyrdom," 629.

3. Ludwig Ott, *Fundamentals of Catholic Dogma* (Rockford, IL: Tan, 1974), 357.

4. Otto Semmelroth, "Martyrdom," in *Encyclopedia of Theology: A Concise Sacramentum Mundi*, ed. Karl Rahner (London: Burns & Oates, 1975), 419, 2(b).

5. Melito of Sardis, *On Pascha and Fragments* (Oxford: Clarendon, 1979). Fragment 12, 79.

6. Tertullian, *De baptismo*, no. 16, in *The Ante-Nicene Fathers*, vol. 3, ed. Alexander Roberts, James Donaldson, and A. Cleveland Coxe (Buffalo, NY: Christian Literature Publishing Company, 1885). See http://www.newadvent.org/fathers/0321.htm. Tertullian's teaching that martyrdom can restore the grace and status of sacramental baptism is highly significant and will be revisited.

7. Cyprian of Carthage, *Epistle 72: To Jubianus*, no. 22.

8. Hippolytus of Rome, *Apostolic Tradition of Hippolytus* (Cambridge: CUP, 1934), no. 19.

9. Ignatius of Antioch, "Epistle to the Romans," nos. 3, 4, in *The Ante-Nicene Fathers*, vol. 1, eds. Alexander Roberts, James Donaldson, and A. Cleveland Coxe (Buffalo, NY: Christian Literature Publishing Company, 1885). See http://www.newadvent.org/fathers/0107.htm.

10. Karl Rahner, "Ignatian Mysticism of Joy in the World," in *Theological Investigations Volume Three: Theology of the Spiritual Life* (London: Darton, Longman & Todd, 1967), 282.

11. Second Vatican Council, *Lumen Gentium* (Dogmatic Constitution on the Church), November 21, 1964, http://www.vatican.va/archive/hist_councils/ii_vatican_council/documents/vat-ii_const_19641121_lumen-gentium_en.html.

12. Karl Rahner, *On the Theology of Death* (Edinburgh: Nelson, 1961), 110, 112.

13. Craig Hovey, *To Share in the Body: A Theology of Martyrdom for Today's Church* (Grand Rapids, MI: Brazos, 2008), 19.

14. Hovey, *To Share in the Body*, 27–28.

15. Augustine of Hippo, "Exposition of Psalm 35," no. 24, in *Nicene and Post-Nicene Fathers, First Series*, vol. 8, ed. Philip

Schaff (Buffalo, NY: Christian Literature Publishing Co., 1888).
See http://www.newadvent.org/fathers/1801035.htm. Augustine
repeats this teaching precisely on at least two other occasions, in
Letters 204 and 185.

16. Cyprian of Carthage, "On the Unity of the Church," no.
14, in *The Ante-Nicene Fathers*, vol. 5. See http://www.newadvent
.org/fathers/050701.htm.

17. Fulgentius of Ruspe, *De Fide ad Petrum*, c.39, n.80, Migne
PL 65, 704: "Firmissime tene, et nullatenus dubites, quemlibet
haereticum sive schismaticum, in nomine Patris et Filii et Spiri-
tus Sancti baptizatum, si Ecclesiae catholicae non fuerit aggrega-
tus, quantascunque eleemosynas fecerit, etsi pro Christi nomine
etiam sanguinem fuderit, nullatenus posse salvari. Omni enim
homini qui Ecclesiae catholicae non tenet unitatem, neque bap-
tismus, neque eleemosyna quamlibet copiosa, neque mors pro
nomine Christi suscepta proficere poterit ad salutem, quando in
eo vel haeretica vel schismatica pravitas perseverat quae ducit ad
mortem."

18. Synod of Laodicea, canon no. 34, in *Nicene and Post-
Nicene Fathers: Second Series*, vol. 14, eds. Philip Schaff and Henry
Wace (Buffalo, NY: Christian Literature Publishing Co, 1900).
See http://www.newadvent.org/fathers/3806.htm.

19. General Council of Florence, "Decree for the Copts,"
in *The Christian Faith in the Doctrinal Documents of the Catholic
Church*, ed. Jacques Dupuis (New York: Alba House, 2001), no.
1005, 421.

3. A DEVELOPING DOCTRINE

1. Louis de Naurois, "Ecclesiastical Penalties," in Rahner,
Encyclopedia, no. 5, 413–14.

2. *CIC*, no. 1364, §1.

3. de Naurois, "Ecclesiastical Penalties," no. 1, 411.

4. *CIC*, no. 1364, §§1 and 2.

5. *CIC*, no. 751.

6. John P. Beal, James A. Coriden, and Thomas J. Green, *New Commentary on the Code of Canon Law* (New York: Paulist Press, 2000), 915.

7. Edward Idris Cassidy, *Ecumenism and Interreligious Dialogue: Unitatis Redintegratio, Nostra Aetate* (New York: Paulist Press, 2005), 13.

8. "Les faux martyrs hérétiques ou schismatiques," R. Hedde, "Martyre II: Notion canonique d'après Benoît XIV," in *Dictionnaire de Théologie Catholique*, Tome 10, Partie 1, ed. A. Vacant and E. Mangenot (Paris: Librairie Letouzey et Ané, 1928), 9, col. 233.

9. "Le second cas est le plus intéressant." Hedde, "Martyre II," col. 233.

10. Prospero Lambertini, *De Servorum Dei Beatificatione et Beatorum Canonizatione*, ed. Emmanuel de Azavedo, 1840.

11. "Il le sera *coram Deo*, pourvu qu'il soit habituellement disposée croire tout ce qui lui serait proposé par l'autorité légitime, car il n'est pas coupable d'après la parole de saint Jean: *Si non venissem et locutus fuissem eis, peccatum non haberent*, XV, 22; il ne le serait pas *coram Ecclesia* qui ne juge que de l'extérieur, et qui, constatant l'hérésie externe, en est réduite à conjecturer l'hérésie interne." Hedde, "Martyr II," col. 233.

12. "On voit par ces exemples combien la notion du martyre qui semble, à première vue, très claire et nettement délimitée, pose en réalité de nombreuses questions auxquelles il est difficile de répondre avec certitude."

13. Thomas Aquinas, *Summa Theologica*, Ia-IIae, q.76, a.2. Conversely *vincible* ignorance he considers a sin of omission in failing to know what one is bound to know and could have known.

14. "Outside of the Church, nobody can hope for life or salvation unless he is excused through ignorance beyond his control." Pius IX, *Singulari Quidem*, March 17, 1856, no. 7.

15. "There are, of course, those who are struggling with invincible ignorance about our most holy religion. Sincerely observing the natural law and its precepts inscribed by God on

all hearts and ready to obey God, they live honest lives and are able to attain eternal life by the efficacious virtue of divine light and grace." Pius IX, *Quanto Conficiamur Moerore*, August 10, 1863, no. 7, http://www.papalencyclicals.net/Pius09/p9quanto.htm.

16. Stephen Bullivant, *The Salvation of Atheists and Catholic Dogmatic Theology* (Oxford: OUP, 2012), 141.

17. Stephen Bullivant, "*Sine culpa?* Vatican II and Inculpable Ignorance," *Theological Studies* (2011): 72.

18. Hedde, "Martyr II," col. 233.

19. "Martyrium vero testimonium fidei divinæ significat et est voluntaria mortis tolerantia propter Christi fidem, vel alium virtutis actum, relatum in Deum." Lambertini, *De Servorum*, III, XI, 1, 118.

20. "Et mentione digni sunt alii etiam, qui, anglicana instituta religiosa profitentes, pro Christi nomine morte affecti sunt." Paul VI, "Homilia in Sollemni Canonizatione Beatorum," October 18, 1964.

21. "His autem addendus esset duplex ac longus index aliorum, qui eadem in cruenta persecutione interempti fuerunt, scilicet alter index neophytos et catechumenos catholicos complectens, alter anglicanos, qui et ipsi - prout narratur - nominis Christi causa sunt necati." Paul VI, "Homilia in Sollemni Canonizatione Beatorum."

22. John Paul II, *Tertio Millennio Adveniente*, November 10, 1994 (emphasis original).

23. John Paul II, *Ut unum sint*, May 25, 1995 (emphasis original).

24. The scope of the generosity expressed here should not be read as extending beyond the invincible/inculpable heretic; the invincibly ignorant are a separate consideration. There is no suggestion of an "anonymous Catholic" analogous to Rahner's anonymous Christian, also inculpable, who can be saved by Christ without having heard the gospel. This "inculpable atheism" is of a different order to the inculpable non-Catholic Christian whose Christianity is established and in whose own church are many of the elements of saving grace identified by the council and John

Paul II. Cf. Karl Rahner, "Anonymous Christians," *Theological Investigations*, vol. 6, *Concerning Vatican Council II* (London: Darton, Longman & Todd, 1969), 397.

25. Cf. Hedde, "Martyr II," col. 233.

4. THE SACRAMENTALITY OF BLOOD

1. "The catechetical tradition also recalls that there are 'sins that cry to heaven': the blood of Abel, the sin of the Sodomites, the cry of the people oppressed in Egypt, the cry of the foreigner, the widow, and the orphan, injustice to the wage earner" (*CCC*, no. 1867).

2. Clement of Alexandria, *Paedagogus*, I, 6, in *The Ante-Nicene Fathers*, vol. 2, eds. Alexander Roberts, James Donaldson, and A. Cleveland Coxe (Buffalo, NY: Christian Literature Publishing Company, 1885).

3. The prohibition on consuming blood is repeated in Lev 3:17 and 7:26.

4. For example, in Acts 15:29.

5. Scott Hahn, *The Lamb's Supper: The Mass as Heaven on Earth* (New York: Doubleday, 1999), 19.

6. "The Holy Sacrifice, because it makes present the one sacrifice of Christ the Savior and includes the Church's offering. The terms holy sacrifice of the Mass, 'sacrifice of praise,' spiritual sacrifice, pure and holy sacrifice are also used, since it completes and surpasses all the sacrifices of the Old Covenant" (*CCC*, no.1330).

7. Cf. Col 2:11–12. See also *Summa Theologiae*, III, 70, 1; and Innocent III, "Letter to Humbert," in *The Christian Faith in the Doctrinal Documents of the Catholic Church*, ed. Jacques Dupuis (New York: Alba House, 2001), no. 1409, 582.

8. Benedict XVI, Post-Synodal Apostolic Exhortation *Sacramentum Caritatis*, February 22, 2007.

9. Joseph Ratzinger, *Collected Works*, vol. 11, *Theology of the Liturgy* (San Francisco: Ignatius Press, 2014), 348.

10. Catholic canon law (no. 844, §§3–4) allows for the baptized not in "full communion" to receive absolution (and anointing and the Eucharist) if in danger of death and who cannot approach their own ministers, and to those of the "Eastern Churches" or churches of equivalent faith who are sick, provided in both cases they "manifest Catholic faith with respect to these sacraments and are properly disposed." Canon 671 of the canon law for Eastern Catholic churches is even more generous regarding such concessions to non-Catholic Eastern churches. These are pastoral concessions made in cases of serious need for individuals. By their nature, they are not intended as public acts, and are conceded for the sake of the salvation of souls. The concession makes sense considering the Catholic teaching since Vatican II that validly baptized non-Catholics are by right members of the Catholic church by their baptism, even if that right has been forsaken thereafter. Martyrdom is, however, an act of public witness to Christ before the world and has an added ecclesial significance (cf. Beal, *New Commentary*, 1024–27).

11. *CCC*, nos. 1440, 1445, 1446 (emphasis original).

12. Cf. Karl Rahner, "The History of Penance," in *Theological Investigations*, vol. 15, *Penance in the Early Church* (London: Darton, Longman & Todd, 1983), 10–12.

13. Council of Elvira, Canon 22, in W. A. Jurgens, *The Faith of the Early Fathers* (Collegeville: Liturgical Press, 1970), 1:255.

14. Tertullian, *De baptismo*, no. 16, in *The Ante-Nicene Fathers*, vol. 3, ed. Alexander Roberts, James Donaldson, and A. Cleveland Coxe (Buffalo, NY: Christian Literature Publishing Company, 1885).

15. Tertullian, *De baptismo*, no. 15.

16. Stephen I, "Letter to Cyprian, Bishop of Carthage," in Dupuis, *Christian Faith*, no. 1401, 579.

17. Innocent I, *Etsi tibi*, in Henry Denziger, *The Sources of Catholic Dogma*, 30th ed. (Fitzwilliam, NH: Loreto, 2002), no. 94, 41.

18. Gregory II, *Desiderabilem mihi*, in Denziger, *Sources*, no. 296a, 118.

19. Council of Nicaea, Canon 8, in Denziger, *Sources*, no. 55, 26.

20. Council of Trent, Seventh Session—March 3, 1547, Canon 4 on Baptism, in Denziger, *Sources*, no. 860, 263.

21. General Council of Florence, *Decree for the Armenians* (1439), in Dupuis, *Christian Faith*, no. 1414, 584.

22. This understanding is accepted in the Articles of Religion (1563) of the Church of England. Note especially no. 26, which is titled "Of the unworthiness of the ministers, which hinders not the effect of the sacrament."

23. Confirmation, or chrismation in the Eastern churches, is one of the three sacraments of full initiation into the church; "[the people of God]...are more perfectly bound to the Church by the sacrament of Confirmation, and the Holy Spirit endows them with special strength so that they are more strictly obliged to spread and defend the faith, both by word and by deed, as true witnesses of Christ" (*Lumen Gentium* 11).

24. Council of Elvira, Canon 38, in Dupuis, *Christian Faith*, no. 1402, 579.

25. Siricius, "Letter to Himerius," in Dupuis, *Christian Faith*, no. 1404, 580.

26. Council of Arelas, Canon 8, in Denziger, *Sources*, no. 53, 25.

27. Cyprian of Carthage, Epistle 11, no. 2, in *The Ante-Nicene Fathers*, vol. 5.

28. Cyprian of Carthage, Epistle 13, no. 2.

29. Third Council of Toledo, Capitulum 11, in Charles Joseph Hefele, *A History of the Councils of the Church*, vol. 4 (Edinburgh: Clark, 1895).

30. Jurgens, *Faith of the Early Fathers*, 244n1–2.

31. Karl Rahner, "Sin as Loss of Grace in Early Church Literature," in *Theological Investigations*, 15:48–49.

32. Cf. *CCC*, nos. 1425–26.

33. Melito of Sardis, *On Pascha and Fragments*, Fragment 12.

34. Semmelroth, "Martyrdom," 419, 2(b).

35. *Summa Theologiae*, III, 66, 12.

36. *CCC*, no. 1272 (emphasis original).

37. Ludwig Ott, *Fundamentals of Catholic Dogma* (Rockford, IL: Tan, 1974), 356.

38. Ott, *Fundamentals*, 356.

39. *CCC*, no. 1273.

40. Ratzinger, *Collected Works*, 348.

41. In other words, "in the realm where the Church exists as a sign of God's kingship on earth." Semmelroth, "Martyrdom," 419, 2(b).

42. Karl Rahner, *On the Theology of Death* (Edinburgh: Nelson, 1961), 110–11.

5. APPLYING RECONCILIATION BY BLOOD

1. Cf. Stomachosus, "Can Non-Catholics Be Martyrs?" February 18, 2015, https://thejosias.com/2015/02/18/dubium-can -non-catholics-be-martyrs/. For something from the peripheries of the Catholic church, see *Novus Ordo Watch*, "It's Heresy: Francis' Ecumenism of Blood Is More Dangerous than ISIS," February 17, 2015, http://www.novusordowatch.org/wire/ecumenism-of -blood-isis.htm.

2. *Hairesis* (Gk.), meaning "choice" or "thing chosen."

3. *Schisma* (Gk.), meaning "split" or "division."

4. *Contumācia* (Lat.), meaning "inflexibility," "arrogance," or "stubbornness." See *CIC*, no. 1364.

5. The baptism of infants and children is implied in the New Testament (e.g., Acts 16:15, where a "household" is baptized), is specifically catered for by Hippolytus ("And first baptize the little ones; if they can speak for themselves, they shall do so; if not, their parents or other relatives shall speak for them." *Apostolic Tradition*, 21:4–5). With the establishment of the doctrine of original sin by Augustine, infant baptism became not only permissible but desirable (cf. Augustine of Hippo, *On Baptism, Against the*

Donatists, IV, 24; and *On Merit and the Forgiveness of Sins, and the Baptism of Infants*, III, 22).

6. See Pew Research Center, "How Many Christians Are There in Egypt?" February 16, 2011, http://www.pewresearch .org/2011/02/16/how-many-christians-are-there-in-egypt/. Also see Central Intelligence Agency, *The World Factbook—Egypt*, August 25, 2016, https://www.cia.gov/library/publications/the -world-factbook/geos/eg.html.

7. The heresy of Nestorius (†450), developed in reaction to the title *Theotokos*, "God-bearer," that was applied to Mary. He rejected that a human could be "mother" of God in his attempt to make sense of the incarnation of God as man. Nestorius proposed that in Christ there were two persons, *hypostases*, one human and the other divine, and that Mary was bearer of the human *hypostasis* Christ, and so she should be called *Christotokos*. Nestorianism was condemned by the Council of Ephesus in 431. See Richard McBrien, *Catholicism* (San Francisco: Harper & Row, 1981), 449–55.

8. The heresy of Eutyches (†456) was a reaction to Nestorianism. It was variously formulated but essentially maintains the unity of Christ by emphasizing his divinity to the point that, in one formulation, Christ's divinity consumed his humanity as the sea consumes a drop of vinegar. It was condemned by the Council of Chalcedon in 451. See McBrien, *Catholicism*, 453–55.

9. Aidan Nichols, *Rome and the Eastern Churches: A Study in Schism*, 2nd ed. (San Francisco: Ignatius, 2010), 84ff. Also see Henry Chadwick, *East and West: The Making of a Rift in the Church* (Oxford: OUP, 2003), 40–49.

10. Nichols, *Rome*, 90–91.

11. Council of Chalcedon, "The Symbol of Chalcedon."

12. Nichols, *Rome*, 95–103.

13. Nichols, *Rome*, 104.

14. Nichols, *Rome*, 105.

15. Nichols, *Rome*, 105.

16. *CIC*, no. 844, §§2 and 3.

17. Pro Oriente, "The Vienna Christological Formula," 1971.

18. Paulos Gregorios (Metropolitan), "The Christological Consensus Reached in Vienna," in *Five Vienna Consultations between Theologians of the Oriental Churches and the Roman Catholic Church 1971, 1973, 1976, 1978 and 1988*, ed. A. Stirnemann and G. Wilflinger (Vienna: Pro Oriente, 1993), 178.

19. "Non-Chalcedonian" churches are those that rejected the settlement achieved by the Council of Chalcedon in 451 regarding the nature of Christ and accept only the first three ecumenical councils. It is synonymous with "Oriental" when used of a church and is used as an explanatory gloss to highlight the source of the separation of the Oriental churches from the Catholic and Orthodox churches.

20. *Common Declaration by Pope Paul VI and His Holiness Mar Ignatius Jacob III*, October 25, 1971, http://www.vatican.va/roman_curia/pontifical_councils/chrstuni/anc-orient-ch-docs/rc_pc_christuni_doc_19711025_syrian-church_en.html.

21. *Common Declaration of Pope Paul VI and of the Pope of Alexandria Shenouda III*, May 10, 1973, http://www.vatican.va/roman_curia/pontifical_councils/chrstuni/anc-orient-ch-docs/rc_pc_christuni_doc_19730510_copti_en.html.

22. A comparable body would be ARCIC (the Anglican-Roman Catholic International Commission). Of a larger scale than the Catholic-Coptic commission, it produces substantial documents outlining areas of agreement and disagreement. Its conclusions have no doctrinal authority per se in the respective member churches though they may influence official doctrinal statements. The Catholic-Coptic commission has issued brief declarations of common faith that are later echoed in the joint declarations by the leaders of the two churches, and to that extent their statements are significant.

23. International Joint Commission between the Catholic Church and the Coptic Orthodox Churches, *Christological Declaration*, August 29, 1976, http://www.prounione.urbe.it/dia-int/oo-rc_copt/doc/e_oo-rc_copt_1976cd.html.

24. *Common Declaration of Pope John Paul II and His Holiness Mar Ignatius Zakka I Iwas*, June 23, 1984, nos. 2–4, 10, http://www.vatican.va/roman_curia/pontifical_councils/chrstuni/anc-orient-ch-docs/rc_pc_christuni_doc_19840623_jp-ii-zakka-i_en.html.

25. International Joint Commission between the Catholic Church and the Coptic Orthodox Churches, *Report and the Brief Formula*, February 12, 1988.

26. The last meeting is listed as April–May 1993. See http://www.prounione.urbe.it/dia-int/oo-rc_copt/e_oo-rc_copt-info.html.

27. See http://www.vatican.va/roman_curia/pontifical_councils/chrstuni/anc-orient-ch-docs/rc_pc_christuni_doc_20030129_prep-meeting_en.html.

28. See various reports at http://www.vatican.va/roman_curia/pontifical_councils/chrstuni/sub-index/index_ancient-oriental-ch.htm.

29. International Joint Commission for Theological Dialogue between the Catholic Church and the Oriental Orthodox Churches, "The Exercise of Communion in the Life of the Early Church and Its Implications for Our Search for Communion Today," May 13, 2015, no. 41.

30. International Joint Commission for Theological Dialogue between the Catholic Church and the Oriental Orthodox Churches, "Report Thirteenth Meeting," February 6, 2016, http://www.vatican.va/roman_curia/pontifical_councils/chrstuni/anc-orient-ch-docs/rc_pc_christuni_doc_20160206_thirteenth-meeting_en.html.

6. EQUIVALENT CANONIZATION

1. *CCC*, no. 828, quoting John Paul II, *Christifideles Laici* (1988), no. 16.

2. *CCC*, nos. 946–62.

3. For example, "To the saints who are...faithful in Christ Jesus" (Eph 1:1); and "To the church of God that is in Corinth, including all the saints throughout Achaia" (2 Cor 1:1).

4. Kenneth L. Woodward, *Making Saints: How the Catholic Church Determines Who Becomes a Saint, Who Doesn't, and Why* (New York: Touchstone, 1996), 55–56.

5. Cf. Camillo Beccari, "Beatification and Canonization," in *The Catholic Encyclopedia*, vol. 2 (New York: Robert Appleton Company, 1907).

6. Woodward, *Making Saints*, 51.

7. See Cyprian, Epistle 8, *Ante-Nicene Fathers*, vol. 5.

8. Woodward, *Making Saints*, 62.

9. Woodward, *Making Saints*, 65.

10. Woodward, *Making Saints*, 66.

11. The process is described in detail in "The Process of Beatification and Canonization" found at https://www.ewtn.com/johnpaul2/cause/process.asp.

12. John Paul II, *Apostolic Constitution Divinus Perfectionis Magister*, January 25, 1983.

13. Beccari, "Beatification and Canonization."

14. "Decrees of the Congregation of the Causes of Saints, May 10, 2012."

15. David Kerr, "Pope Benedict Creates Two New Doctors of the Church," *Catholic News Agency*, October 7, 2012, http://www.catholicnewsagency.com/news/pope-benedict-creates-two-new-doctors-of-the-church/.

16. "Decrees of the Congregation of the Causes of Saints, October 11, 2013."

17. "Decrees of the Congregation of the Causes of Saints, December 17, 2013."

18. "La virtù di perdere tempo," *L'Osservatore Romano*, December 21, 2013.

19. "Pope Francis Declares Armenian Saint Doctor of the Church," *Vatican Radio*, February 23, 2015, https://zenit.org/articles/saint-gregory-of-narek-declared-doctor-of-the-universal-church/.

20. *Joint Declaration of Paul VI and Vasken I, Supreme Catholicos-Patriarch of All Armenians*, May 12, 1970, http://www.vatican.va/roman_curia/pontifical_councils/chrstuni/anc-orient-ch-docs/rc_pc_christuni_doc_19700512_joint-decl_en.html.

21. *Common Declaration of John Paul II and Catholicos Karekin I*, December 13, 1996, http://www.vatican.va/roman_curia/pontifical_councils/chrstuni/anc-orient-ch-docs/rc_pc_christuni_doc_19961213_jp-ii-karekin-i_en.html.

22. *Joint Declaration of John Paul II and Catholicos Karekin II*, November 10, 2000, http://www.ewtn.com/library/PAPALDOC/ZJP2ARMN.HTM.

23. Aidan Nichols, *Rome and the Eastern Churches: A Study in Schism*, 2nd ed. (San Francisco: Ignatius, 2010), 121.

24. Nichols, *Rome*, 122.

25. Nichols, *Rome*, 134.

26. See John Paul II, *Divinis Perfectionis Magister*, I, no. 1.

27. See "Gregory of Narek Is Declared a Doctor of the Church," *La Stampa*, February 23, 2015, http://www.lastampa.it/2015/02/23/esteri/vatican-insider/en/gregory-of-narek-is-declared-a-doctor-of-the-church-9Ufk3jmUDjz7OFondodZgI/pagina.html.

28. "Message of Catholicos Karekin II," *Vatican Radio*, April 12, 2015, https://zenit.org/articles/message-of-catholicos-of-all-armenians-his-holiness-karekin-ii/.

29. "Armenian Catholicos Karekin at Divine Liturgy in Etchmiadzin," *Vatican Radio*, June 26, 2016, https://zenit.org/articles/message-of-his-holiness-karekin-ii-catholicos-of-all-armenians-during-divine-liturgy/.

30. "Pope Francis in Armenia: May We Hasten to Christian Unity," *Vatican Radio*, June 26, 2016, https://zenit.org/articles/may-we-follow-gods-call-to-full-communion-and-hasten-towards-it-says-pope/.

31. *Joint Declaration by Pope Francis and the Catholicos Karekin II*, June 26, 2016, https://press.vatican.va/content/salastampa/en/bollettino/pubblico/2016/06/27/160627d.html.

32. "Coptic Church Recognizes Martyrdom," *Vatican Radio*,

February 21, 2015, https://zenit.org/articles/martyrdom-of-21 -egyptian-coptic-christians-recognized-by-coptic-church/.

33. "ACN Press Release—Egypt 'The Church Has Been Strengthened,'" February 19, 2015, https://acn-canada.org/acn -press-release-egypt-the-church-has-been-strengthened/.

34. "ACN News—Egypt 'They Are True Martyrs,'" March 24, 2015, https://acn-canada.org/acn-news-egypt-they-are-true -martyrs/.

35. "Pope Sends Letter to Coptic Patriarch on Day of Friendship," *Vatican Radio*, May 10, 2016, https://zenit.org/articles/ pope-sends-message-to-pope-tawadros-ii-of-alexandria-2/.

7. CONCLUSION

1. *Common Declaration of His Holiness Francis and His Holiness Tawadros II*, April 28, 2017, no. 2, http://w2.vatican.va/content/ francesco/en/speeches/2017/april/documents/papa-francesco _20170428_egitto-tawadros-ii.html#Common_Declaration.

2. *Common Declaration*, no. 11.

3. *Common Declaration*, no. 2. For the author, there is the satisfaction that he makes this proposal as a son of St. Benedict, who established in the west the cenobitic monasticism pioneered by St. Pachomius of Egypt, and obliquely referred to by the two popes as an element of their ancient communion.

Bibliography

Aid to the Church in Need. "ACN Press Release—Egypt 'The Church Has Been Strengthened.'" February 19, 2015. https://acn-canada.org/acn-press-release-egypt-the-church -has-been-strengthened/.

———. "ACN News—Egypt 'They Are True Martyrs.'" March 24, 2015. https://acn-canada.org/acn-news-egypt-they-are -true-martyrs/.

Aquinas, Thomas. The "Summa Theologica" of St. Thomas Aquinas. Second and revised edition. London: Burns Oates and Washbourne, 1920. Translated by Fathers of the English Dominican Province. Online edition by Kevin Knight, 2017. http://www.newadvent.org/summa/index.html.

"Armenian Catholicos Karekin at Divine Liturgy in Etchmiadzin," Vatican Radio, June 26, 2016. https://zenit.org/articles/ message-of-his-holiness-karekin-ii-catholicos-of-all -armenians-during-divine-liturgy/.

Bartholomew I. "Address of the Ecumenical Patriarch Bartholomew I to Pope Francis." November 30, 2014. https://www.patriarchate.org/-/address-by-his-all-holiness -ecumenical-patriarch-bartholomew-to-his-holiness-pope -francis-during-the-divine-liturgy-for-the-feast-of-st -andrew-in-the-.

Beal, John P., James A. Coriden, and Thomas J. Green. *New Commentary on the Code of Canon Law*. New York: Paulist Press, 2000.

Beccari, Camillo. "Beatification and Canonization." In *The Catholic Encyclopedia*, vol. 2. New York: Robert Appleton Company, 1907. http://www.newadvent.org/cathen/023 64b.htm.

Benedict XVI. Post-Synodal Apostolic Exhortation *Sacramentum caritatis*, February 22, 2007. http://w2.vatican.va/content/ benedict-xvi/en/apost_exhortations/documents/hf_ben -xvi_exh_20070222_sacramentum-caritatis.html.

Buchanan, Rose Troup. "Daesh: What Does the Word Mean? Is David Cameron's Use of It Significant?" *The Independent* (UK), December 2, 2015.

Bullivant, Stephen. *The Salvation of Atheists and Catholic Dogmatic Theology*. Oxford: OUP, 2012.

———. "*Sine Culpa?* Vatican II and Inculpable Ignorance." *Theological Studies* 72 (2011): doi:10.1177/004056391107 200104.

Cameron, Rondo. *Concise Economic History of the World*. New York: OUP, 1993.

Cassidy, Edward Idris. *Ecumenism and Interreligious Dialogue: Unitatis Redintegratio, Nostra Aetate*. New York: Paulist Press, 2005.

Catechism of the Catholic Church. New York: Doubleday, 1995.

Center for the Study of Global Christianity. "Global Diagram 16: Evangelization through Martyrdom, 2001." Taken from: Todd M. Johnson, ed. *World Christian Trends*. Leiden/ Boston: Brill, 2001. http://www.gordonconwell.edu/ock enga/research/documents/gd16.pdf.

———. "Martyrdom Situations 2000–2010." Taken from: Todd M. Johnson and Gina A. Zurlo, eds. *World Christian Database*. Leiden/Boston: Brill, 2014. http://www.gordonconwell .edu/ockenga/research/documents/1martyrdomsituations .pdf.

————. "Status of Global Christianity, 2017, in the Context of 1900–2050." Taken from: Todd M. Johnson and Gina A. Zurlo, eds. *World Christian Database*. Leiden/Boston: Brill, 2014. http://www.gordonconwell.edu/ockenga/research/doc uments/StatusofGlobalChristianity2017.pdf.

Central Intelligence Agency. *The World Factbook—Egypt*. August 25, 2016. https://www.cia.gov/library/publications/the-world -factbook/geos/eg.html.

Chadwick, Henry. *East and West: The Making of a Rift in the Church*. Oxford: OUP, 2003.

Chalcedon General Council. "The Symbol of Chalcedon." http:// www.ccel.org/ccel/schaff/creeds2.iv.i.iii.html.

Code of Canon Law (Codex Iuris Canonici) (CIC). Vatican City: Libreria Editrice Vaticana, 1983. http://www.vatican.va/ archive/ENG1104/__P2H.HTM.

"Common Declaration of Pope Paul VI and the Pope of Alexandria Shenouda III," May 10, 1973. http://www.vatican.va/roman _curia/pontifical_councils/chrstuni/anc-orient-ch-docs/rc _pc_christuni_doc_19730510_copti_en.html.

Congregation of the Causes of Saints. "Decrees, May 10, 2012." http://visnews-en.blogspot.co.uk/2012/05/decrees-of -congregation-for-causes-of_11.html.

————. "Decrees, October 11, 2013." http://www.vis.va/ vissolr/index.php?vi=en&dl=e2a47a2e-d5d0-2084-ef7c -5257f8362024&dl_t=text/xml&dl_a=y&ul=1&ev=1.

————. "Decrees, December 17, 2013." http://www.news.va/ en/news/promulgation-of-decrees-of-the-congregation -for-th.

"Coptic Church Recognizes Martyrdom of 21 Coptic Christians." *Vatican Radio*, February 21, 2015. https://zenit.org/articles/ martyrdom-of-21-egyptian-coptic-christians-recognized -by-coptic-church/.

Denziger, Henry. *The Sources of Catholic Dogma*. 30th ed. Fitzwilliam, NH: Loreto, 2002.

Dupuis, Jacques, ed. *The Christian Faith in the Doctrinal Documents of the Catholic Church*. New York: Alba House, 2001.

England, Laurence. "They Didn't Die for Ecumenism," February 16, 2015. http://thatthebonesyouhavecrushedmaythrill.blog spot.co.uk/2015/02/they-didnt-die-for-ecumenism.html.

Eternal Word Television Network. "The Process of Beatification and Canonization." Accessed January 2018, https://www.ewtn.com/johnpaul2/cause/process.asp.

Francis. "Address of His Holiness Pope Francis to Members of the Catholic Fraternity of Charismatic Covenant Communities and Fellowships," October 31, 2014. http://w2.vatican.va/content/francesco/en/speeches/2014/october/documents/papa-francesco_20141031_catholic-fraternity.html.

———. "Address of His Holiness Pope Francis to the Moderator and Representatives of the Church of Scotland," February 16, 2015. http://w2.vatican.va/content/francesco/en/speeches/2015/february/documents/papa-francesco_20150216 _moderatore-chiesa-scozia.html.

———. "Address of His Holiness Pope Francis to the Renewal in the Holy Spirit Movement," St. Peter's Square, July 3, 2015. http://w2.vatican.va/content/francesco/en/speeches/2015/july/documents/papa-francesco_20150703_movimento -rinnovamento-spirito.html.

———. "Address of Pope Francis to His Holiness Karekin II Supreme Patriarch and Catholicos of all Armenians with his Entourage," May 8, 2014. http://w2.vatican.va/content/francesco/en/speeches/2014/may/documents/papa -francesco_20140508_patriarca-armeni.html.

———. "Common Declaration of His Holiness Pope Francis and His Holiness Pope Tawadros II," April 28, 2017. http://w2.vatican.va/content/francesco/en/speeches/2017/april/documents/papa-francesco_20170428_egitto-tawadros-ii .html#Common_Declaration.

———. "Homily of His Holiness Pope Francis at the Celebration of Vespers on the Solemnity of the Conversion of Saint Paul the Apostle," January 25, 2015. http://w2.vatican.va/content/francesco/en/homilies/2015/documents/papa -francesco_20150125_vespri-conversione-san-paolo.html.

————. "Joint Declaration by Pope Francis and the Catholicos Karekin II," June 26, 2016. https://press.vatican.va/content/salastampa/en/bollettino/pubblico/2016/06/27/160627d.html.

————. "Joint Declaration of Pope Francis and Ecumenical Patriarch Bartholomew I," November 30, 2014. https://www.patriarchate.org/-/joint-declaration-of-his-holiness-pope-francis-and-his-all-holiness-ecumenical-patriarch-bartholomew-november-30-2014-.

————. "Message of His Holiness Pope Francis to His Holiness Abuna Matthias Patriarch of the Ethiopian Tewahedo Orthodox Church," April 20, 2015. http://w2.vatican.va/content/francesco/en/messages/pont-messages/2015/documents/papa-francesco_20150420_messaggio-abuna-matthias.html.

————. "Message of His Holiness Pope Francis to His Holiness Tawadros II Pope of Alexandria and Patriarch of the See of Saint Mark," May 10, 2015. http://w2.vatican.va/content/francesco/en/messages/pont-messages/2015/documents/papa-francesco_20150510_messaggio-tawadros-ii.html.

Fulgentius of Ruspe. *De Fide ad Petrum*. J. P. Migne. PL 65:39.

Gagliarducci, Andrea. "Remember the Copts ISIS Martyred in Libya? This Priest Does," July 19, 2016. http://www.catholicnewsagency.com/news/remember-the-copts-isis-martyred-in-libya-this-priest-does-68914/.

"Gregory of Narek Is Declared a Doctor of the Church." *La Stampa*, February 23, 2015. http://www.lastampa.it/2015/02/23/esteri/vatican-insider/en/gregory-of-narek-is-declared-a-doctor-of-the-church-9Ufk3jmUDjz7OFondodZgI/pagina.html.

Hahn, Scott. *The Lamb's Supper: The Mass as Heaven on Earth*. New York: Doubleday, 1999.

Hefele, Charles Joseph. *A History of the Councils of the Church*. vol. 4. Edinburgh: Clark, 1895. http://www.ecatholic2000.com/councils/untitled-48.shtml.

Hippolytus of Rome. *Apostolic Tradition of Hippolytus*. Cambridge: Cambridge University Press, 1934.

Hovey, Craig. *To Share in the Body: A Theology of Martyrdom for Today's Church*. Grand Rapids, MI: Brazos, 2008.

International Joint Commission between the Catholic Church and the Coptic Orthodox Church. *Christological Declaration*, August 29, 1976. http://www.prounione.urbe.it/dia-int/oo -rc_copt/doc/e_oo-rc_copt_1976cd.html.

———. *Common Report and Brief Formula*, February 12, 1988. http://www.prounione.urbe.it/dia-int/oo-rc_copt/doc/e _oo-rc_copt_1988.html.

International Joint Commission for Theological Dialogue between the Catholic Church and the Oriental Orthodox Churches. "The Exercise of Communion in the Life of the Early Church and Its Implications for Our Search for Communion Today," May 13, 2015. http://www.vatican.va/ roman_curia/pontifical_councils/chrstuni/anc-orient-ch -docs/rc_pc_chrstuni_doc_20150513_exercise-communion _en.html.

———. "Report of Thirteenth Meeting," February 6, 2016. http://www.vatican.va/roman_curia/pontifical_coun cils/chrstuni/anc-orient-ch-docs/rc_pc_chrstuni_doc _20160206_thirteenth-meeting_en.html.

"It's Heresy: Francis' 'Ecumenism of Blood.'" *Novus Ordo Watch*, February 17, 2015. http://www.novusordowatch.org/wire/ ecumenism-of-blood-isis.htm.

John Paul II. Apostolic Constitution *Divinus Perfectionis Magister*, January 25, 1983. http://w2.vatican.va/content/john-paul-ii/ en/apost_constitutions/documents/hf_jp-ii_apc_25011983 _divinus-perfectionis-magister.html.

———. Apostolic Letter *Tertio Millennio Adveniente*, November 10, 1994. http://w2.vatican.va/content/john-paul-ii/en/ apost_letters/1994/documents/hf_jp-ii_apl_19941110 _tertio-millennio-adveniente.html.

———. *Common Declaration of John Paul II and Catholicos Karekin I*, December 1996. http://www.vatican.va/roman_curia/ponti

fical_councils/chrstuni/anc-orient-ch-docs/rc_pc _christuni_doc_19961213_jp-ii-karekin-i_en.html.

———. *Common Declaration of Pope John Paul II and His Holiness Mar Ignatius Zakka I Iwas*, June 23, 1984. http://www.vatican .va/roman_curia/pontifical_councils/chrstuni/anc-orient -ch-docs/rc_pc_christuni_doc_19840623_jp-ii-zakka-i_en .html.

———. Encyclical Letter *Ut Unum Sint*, May 25, 1995. http:// w2.vatican.va/content/john-paul-ii/en/encyclicals/ documents/hf_jp-ii_enc_25051995_ut-unum-sint.html.

———. *Joint Declaration of John Paul II and Catholicos Karekin II*, November 10, 2000. http://www.ewtn.com/library/ PAPALDOC/ZJP2ARMN.HTM.

Jurgens, W. A. *The Faith of the Early Fathers*. vol. 1. Collegeville: Liturgical Press, 1970.

Karekin II. "Address of Pope Francis to His Holiness Karekin II Supreme Patriarch and Catholicos of all Armenians with his Entourage," May 8, 2014. http://w2.vatican.va/content/ francesco/en/speeches/2014/may/documents/papa -francesco_20140508_patriarca-armeni.html.

———. "Message of Catholicos Karekin II." *Vatican Radio*, April 12, 2015. https://zenit.org/articles/message-of-catholicos -of-all-armenians-his-holiness-karekin-ii/.

Kerr, David. "Pope Benedict Creates Two New Doctors of the Church," October 7, 2012. http://www.catholicnewsagency .com/news/pope-benedict-creates-two-new-doctors-of-the -church/.

Komonchak, Joseph, Mary Collins, and Dermot Lane, eds. *The New Dictionary of Theology*. Wilmington, DE: Michael Glazier, 1987.

Lambertini, Prospero. *De Servorum Dei Beatificatione et Beatorum Canonizatione*. Edited by Emmanuel de Azavedo, 1840. http://www.miraclehunter.com/marian_apparitions/ discernment/Benedicti_Papae_XIV_Doctrina_de _servorum.pdf.

"La virtù di perdere tempo." *L'Osservatore Romano*, December 21, 2013. http://www.osservatoreromano.va/it/news/la-virtu -di-perdere-tempo.

Maksan, Oliver. "First Fruits of 21 Copts' Martyrdom." *Zenit*, March 24, 2015. https://zenit.org/articles/first-fruits-of-21 -copts-martyrdom/.

Malsin, Jared. "Christians Mourn Their Relatives Beheaded by ISIS." *Time*, February 23, 2015. http://time.com/3718470/ isis-copts-egypt/.

Manning, Patrick. "African Population, 1650–1950: Methods for New Estimates by Region." *African Economic History Conference*, Vancouver, 2013. http://mortenjerven.com/ wp-content/uploads/2013/04/AfricanPopulation.Methods .pdf.

McBrien, Richard. *Catholicism*. San Francisco: Harper & Row, 1981.

Melito of Sardis. *On* Pascha *and Fragments*. Oxford: Clarendon, 1979.

Milco, Elliot. "Can Non-Catholics Be Martyrs?" *The Josias*, February 18, 2015. https://thejosias.com/2015/02/18/dubium-can -non-catholics-be-martyrs/.

Nichols, Aidan. *Rome and the Eastern Churches: A Study in Schism*. 2nd ed. San Francisco: Ignatius, 2010.

Ott, Ludwig. *Common Declaration by Pope Paul VI and His Holiness Mar Ignatius Jacob III*. October 25, 1971. http://www.vatican .va/roman_curia/pontifical_councils/chrstuni/anc-orient -ch-docs/rc_pc_christuni_doc_19711025_syrian-church _en.html.

———. *Common Declaration of Pope Paul VI and of the Pope of Alexandria Shenouda III*, May 10, 1973. http://www.vatican .va/roman_curia/pontifical_councils/chrstuni/anc-orient -ch-docs/rc_pc_christuni_doc_19730510_copti_en.html.

———. *Fundamentals of Catholic Dogma*. Rockford, IL: Tan Books, 1974.

P., Janelle. "Announcing the 2017 World Watch List." *Open Doors USA*, January 11, 2017. https://www.opendoorsusa

.org/christian-persecution/stories/announcing-2017-world
-watch-list/.

Paul VI. "Homilia in Sollemni Canonizatione Beatorum: Caroli
Lwanga, Matthiae Mulumba Kalemba et viginti sociorum
Martyrum Ugandensium," October 18, 1964. http://w2
.vatican.va/content/paul-vi/la/homilies/1964/documents/
hf_p-vi_hom_19641018_martiri-uganda.html.

———. *Joint Declaration of Paul VI and Vasken I, Supreme Catholicos-
Patriarch of All Armenians*, May 12, 1970. http://www.vatican
.va/roman_curia/pontifical_councils/chrstuni/anc-orient
-ch-docs/rc_pc_christuni_doc_19700512_joint-decl_en
.html.

Pew Research Center. "How Many Christians Are There in
Egypt?" February 16, 2011. http://www.pewresearch.org/
2011/02/16/how-many-christians-are-there-in-egypt/.

———. "Trends in Global Restrictions on Religion," Complete
Report, June 23, 2016. http://www.pewforum.org/2016/06/
23/trends-in-global-restrictions-on-religion/.

Pius IX. *Quanto Conficiamur Moerore*, August 10, 1863. http://
www.papalencyclicals.net/Pius09/p9quanto.htm.

———. *Singulari Quidem*, March 17, 1856. http://www
.papalencyclicals.net/Pius09/p9singul.htm.

"Pope Francis Declares Armenian Saint Doctor of the Church."
Vatican Radio, February 23, 2015. https://zenit.org/articles/
saint-gregory-of-narek-declared-doctor-of-the-universal
-church/.

"Pope Francis in Armenia: May We Hasten to Christian Unity."
Vatican Radio, June 26, 2016. https://zenit.org/articles/
may-we-follow-gods-call-to-full-communion-and-hasten
-towards-it-says-pope/.

"Pope Sends Letter to Coptic Patriarch on Day of Friendship."
Vatican Radio, May 10, 2016. https://zenit.org/articles/pope
-sends-message-to-pope-tawadros-ii-of-alexandria-2/.

Pro Oriente. "The Vienna Christological Formula," 1972. http://
www.pro-oriente.at/index.php?site=gl20050201095749.

Rahner, Karl. *Theological Investigations Volume Three: Theology of the Spiritual Life*. London: Darton, Longman & Todd, 1967.

—————. *Theological Investigations Volume Six: Concerning Vatican Council II*. London: Darton, Longman & Todd, 1969.

—————. *Theological Investigations Volume Fifteen: Penance in the Early Church*. London: Darton, Longman & Todd, 1983.

—————, ed. *Encyclopedia of Theology: A Concise Sacramentum Mundi*. London: Burns & Oates, 1975.

—————, ed. *Sacramentum Mundi*, vol. 1. London: Burns & Oates, 1968.

Ratzinger, Joseph. *Collected Works Volume 11: Theology of the Liturgy*. San Francisco: Ignatius, 2014.

Roberts, Alexander, James Donaldson, and A. Cleveland Coxe, eds. *The Ante-Nicene Fathers*. vol. 1. Buffalo, NY: Christian Literature Publishing Company, 1885. http://www.newadvent.org/fathers/index.html.

—————. *The Ante-Nicene Fathers*. vol. 2. Buffalo, NY: Christian Literature Publishing Company, 1885. http://www.newadvent.org/fathers/index.html.

—————. *The Ante-Nicene Fathers*. vol. 3. Buffalo, NY: Christian Literature Publishing Company, 1885. http://www.newadvent.org/fathers/index.html.

—————. *The Ante-Nicene Fathers*. vol. 5. Buffalo, NY: Christian Literature Publishing Company, 1886. http://www.newadvent.org/fathers/index.html.

Scalia, Elizabeth. "Witnesses to Martyrdom: Father Hamel's Last Moments." *Aleteia*, October 4, 2016. http://aleteia.org/2016/10/04/witnesses-to-martyrdom-father-hamels-last-moments/.

Schaff, Philip, ed. *Nicene and Post-Nicene Fathers, First Series*. vol. 8. Buffalo, NY: Christian Literature Publishing Company, 1888. http://www.newadvent.org/fathers/index.html.

Schaff, Philip, and Henry Wace, eds. *Nicene and Post-Nicene Fathers, Second Series*. vol. 14. Buffalo, NY: Christian Literature Publishing Company, 1900. http://www.newadvent.org/fathers/index.html.

Smith, Samuel. "90,000 Christians Killed in 2016, 1 Every 6 Minutes: Study." *Christian Post*, December 30, 2016. https://www.christianpost.com/news/90000-christians-killed-in-2016-1-every-6-minutes-study-172464/.

Somerville-Knapman, Hugh. "Can Catholics Recognize the 21 Murdered Coptic Christians as Martyrs?" *Catholic Herald*, February 24, 2015. http://www.catholicherald.co.uk/commentandblogs/2015/02/24/can-catholics-recognise-the-21-murdered-coptic-christians-as-martyrs/.

Stirnemann, A., and G. Wilflinger, eds. *Five Vienna Consultations between Theologians of the Oriental Churches and the Roman Catholic Church 1971, 1973, 1976, 1978 and 1988*. Vienna: Pro Oriente, 1993.

Strumia, Alberto. "Analogy." *Interdisciplinary Encyclopedia of Religion and Science* (2010). doi:10.17421/2037-2329-2010-AS-1.

Tornielli, Andrea. "Never Be Afraid of Tenderness." *La Stampa: Vatican Insider*, December 2013. http://www.lastampa.it/2013/12/14/esteri/vatican-insider/en/never-be-afraid-of-tenderness-5BqUfVs9r7W1CJIMuHqNeI/pagina.html.

United Nations, Department of Economic and Social Affairs, Population Division. *World Population Prospects: The 2015 Revision*. http://www.worldometers.info/world-population/africa-population/.

U.S. Department of State. "International Religious Freedom Report for 2015." http://www.state.gov/j/drl/rls/irf/religiousfreedom/index.htm?year=2015&dlid=256267.

Vacant, A., and E. Mangenot, eds. *Dictionnaire de Théologie Catholique*. Tome 10, Partie 1. Paris: Librairie Letouzey et Ané, 1928.

Vatican Council II. *Lumen Gentium* (Dogmatic Constitution on the Church), November 21, 1964. http://www.vatican.va/archive/hist_councils/ii_vatican_council/documents/vat-ii_const_19641121_lumen-gentium_en.html.

———. *Unitatis Redintegratio* (Decree on Ecumenism), November 21, 1964. http://www.vatican.va/archive/hist_councils/ii

_vatican_council/documents/vat-ii_decree_19641121 _unitatis-redintegratio_en.html.

Woodward, Kenneth L. *Making Saints: How the Catholic Church Determines Who Becomes a Saint, Who Doesn't, and Why*. New York: Touchstone, 1996.

INDEX